MYTHOLOGY GRAPHICS

BATTLE OF THE TITANS

A MODERN GRAPHIC GREEK MYTH

BY STEPHANIE PETERS

ILLUSTRATED BY MARIAN SLOANE

CAPSTONE PRESS

a capstone imprint

Published by Capstone Press, an imprint of Capstone
1710 Roe Crest Drive, North Mankato, Minnesota 56003
capstonepub.com

Library of Congress Cataloging-in-Publication Data is available
on the Library of Congress website.
ISBN: 9781669059080 (hardcover)
ISBN: 9781669059103 (paperback)
ISBN: 9781669059110 (ebook PDF)

Summary: No one knows family drama like the Titans. And when they go
head-to-head with the Olympians, the battle lasts ten years—and includes
plenty of jealousy and sibling rivalry. Who comes out on top in this epic family
fight for control of the universe? Find out in this modern, graphic retelling of a
classic Greek myth.

Editorial Credits
Editor: Alison Deering; Designer: Jaime Willems;
Production Specialist: Whitney Schaefer

Printed and bound in the USA. PO 5626

TABLE OF CONTENTS

CHAPTER 1

THE UNIVERSE'S FIRST FAMILY FEUD

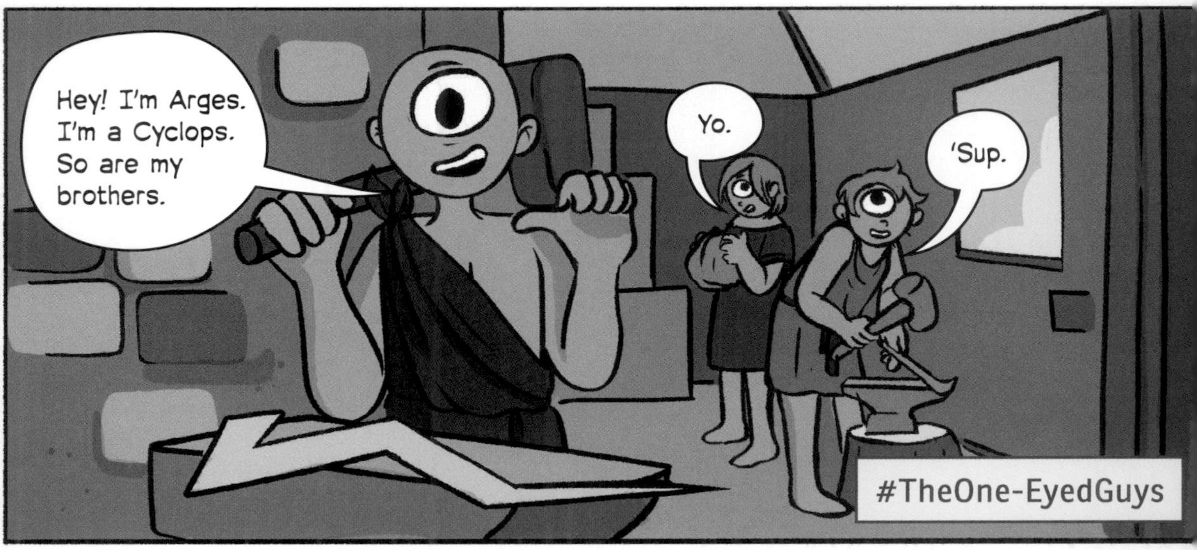
Hey! I'm Arges. I'm a Cyclops. So are my brothers.
Yo.
'Sup.
#TheOne-EyedGuys

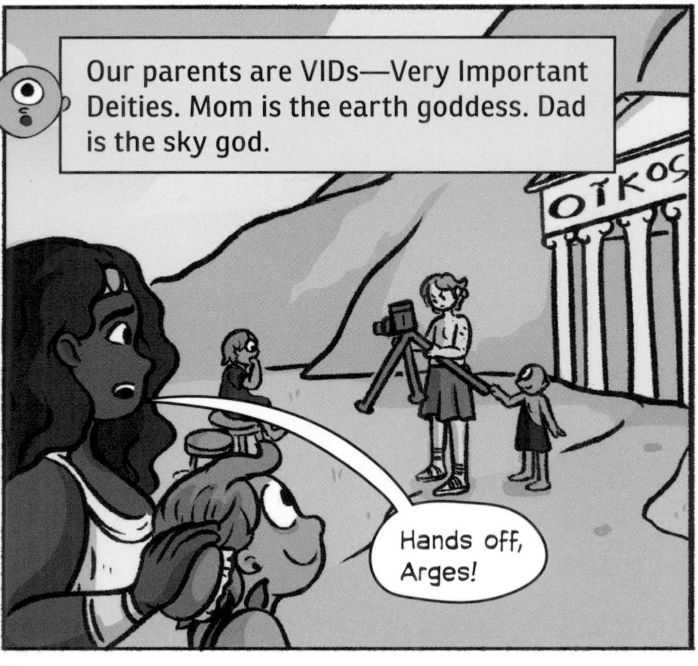
Our parents are VIDs—Very Important Deities. Mom is the earth goddess. Dad is the sky god.
OIKOS
Hands off, Arges!

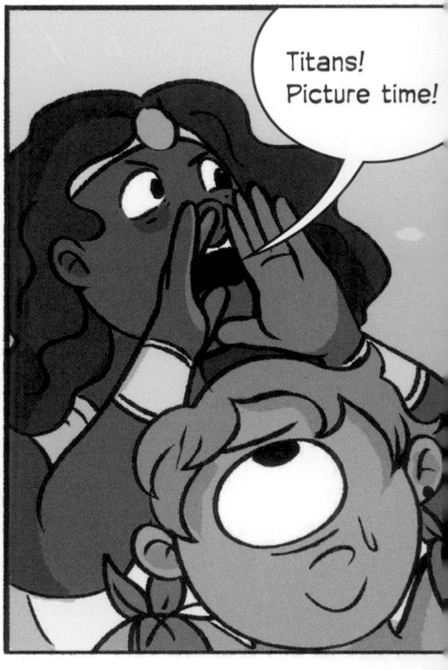
Titans! Picture time!

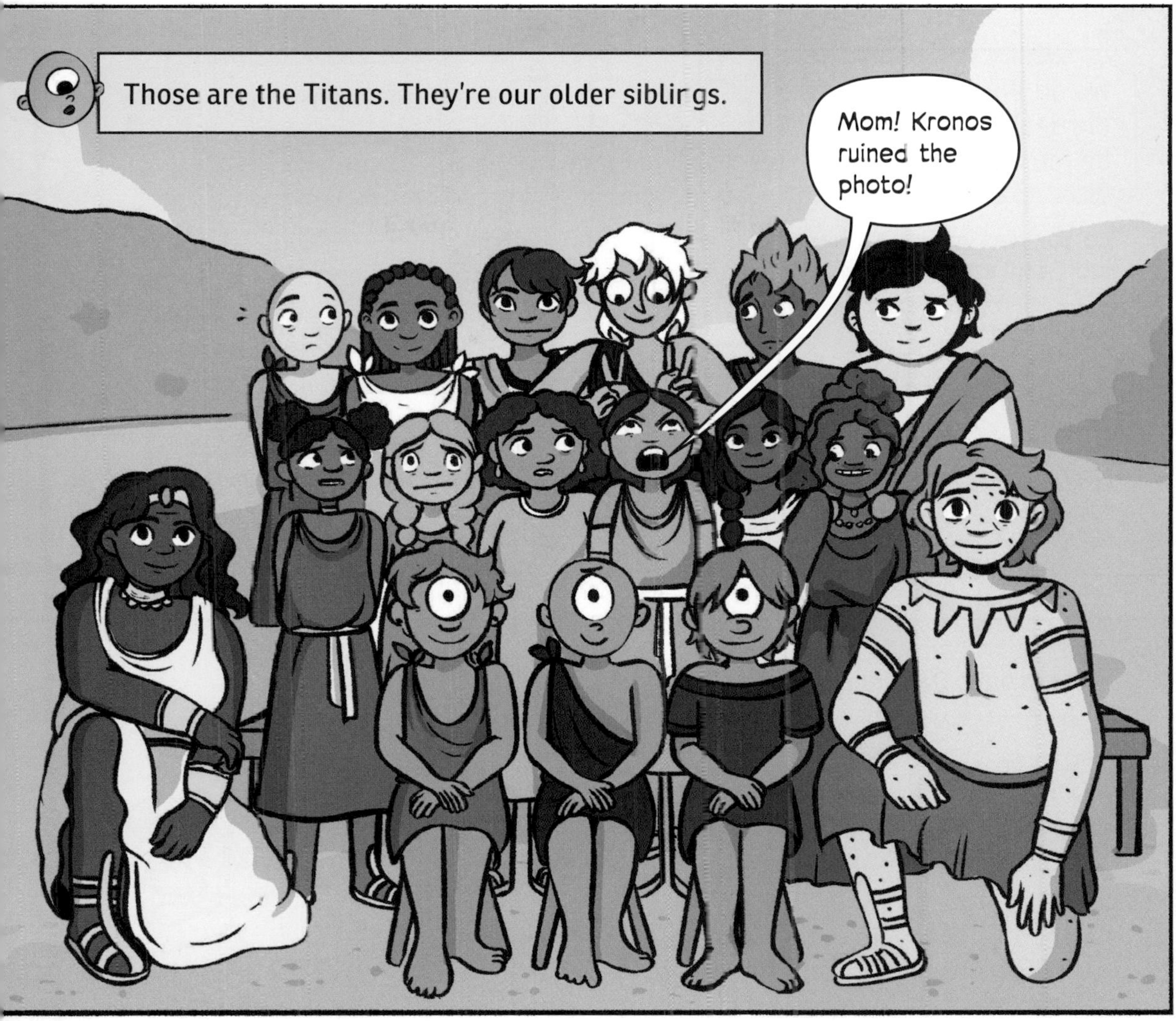
Those are the Titans. They're our older siblings.
Mom! Kronos ruined the photo!

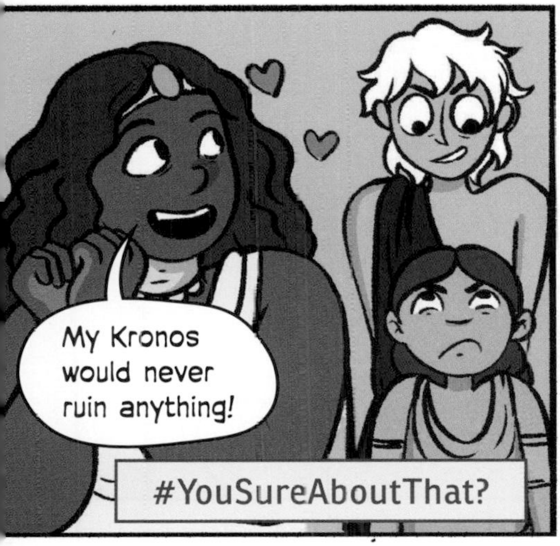
My Kronos would never ruin anything!
#YouSureAboutThat?

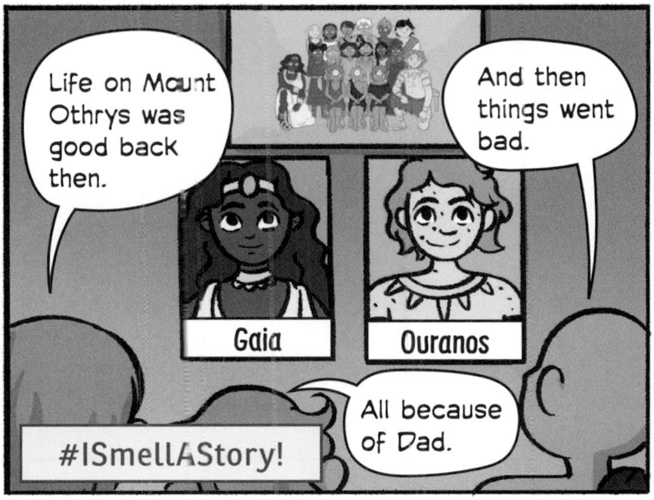
Life on Mount Othrys was good back then.
And then things went bad.
Gaia
Ouranos
All because of Dad.
#ISmellAStory!

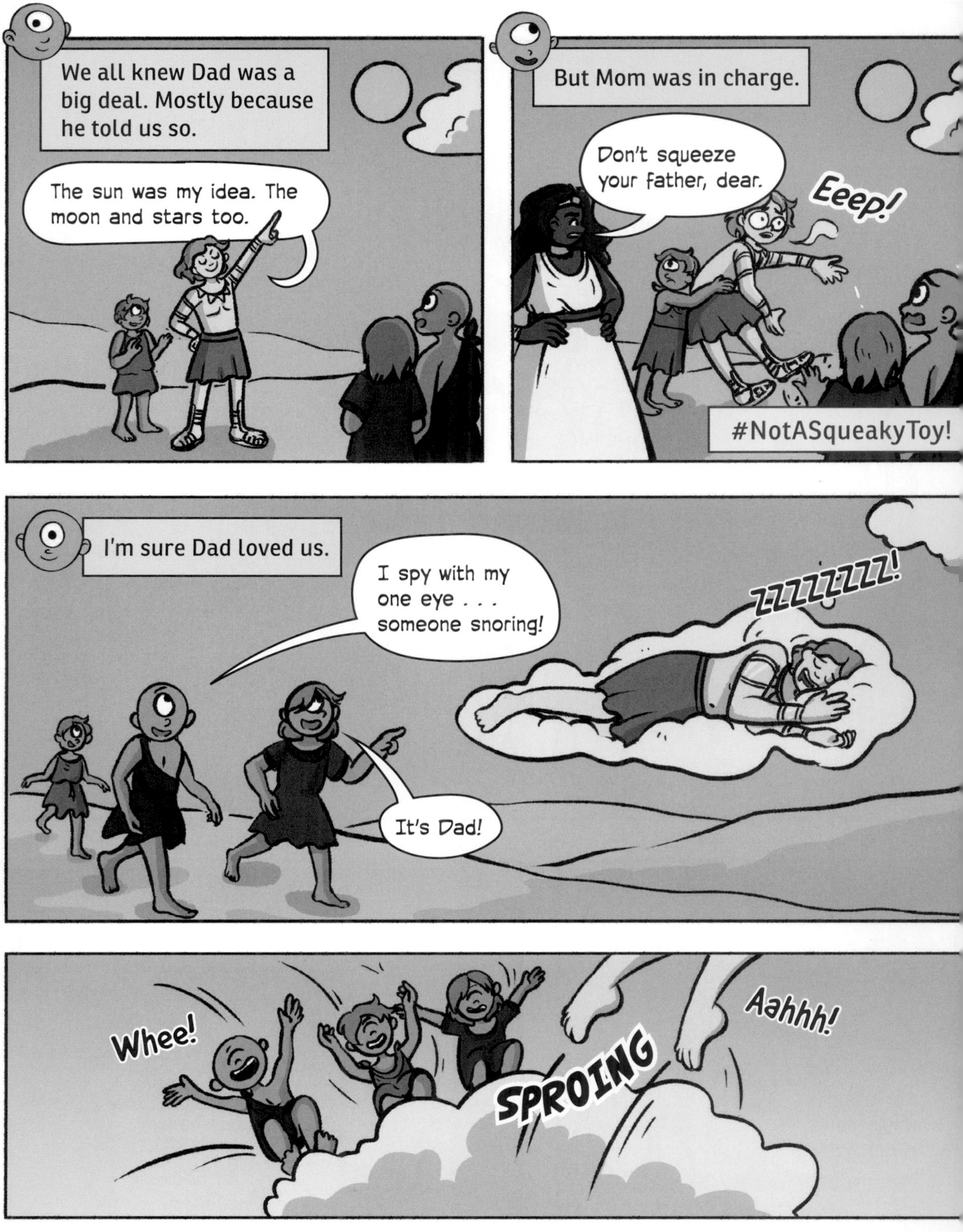

We all knew Dad was a big deal. Mostly because he told us so.
The sun was my idea. The moon and stars too.
But Mom was in charge.
Don't squeeze your father, dear.
Eeep!
#NotASqueakyToy!
I'm sure Dad loved us.
I spy with my one eye . . . someone snoring!
ZZZZZZZZ!
It's Dad!
Whee!
SPROING
Aahhh!

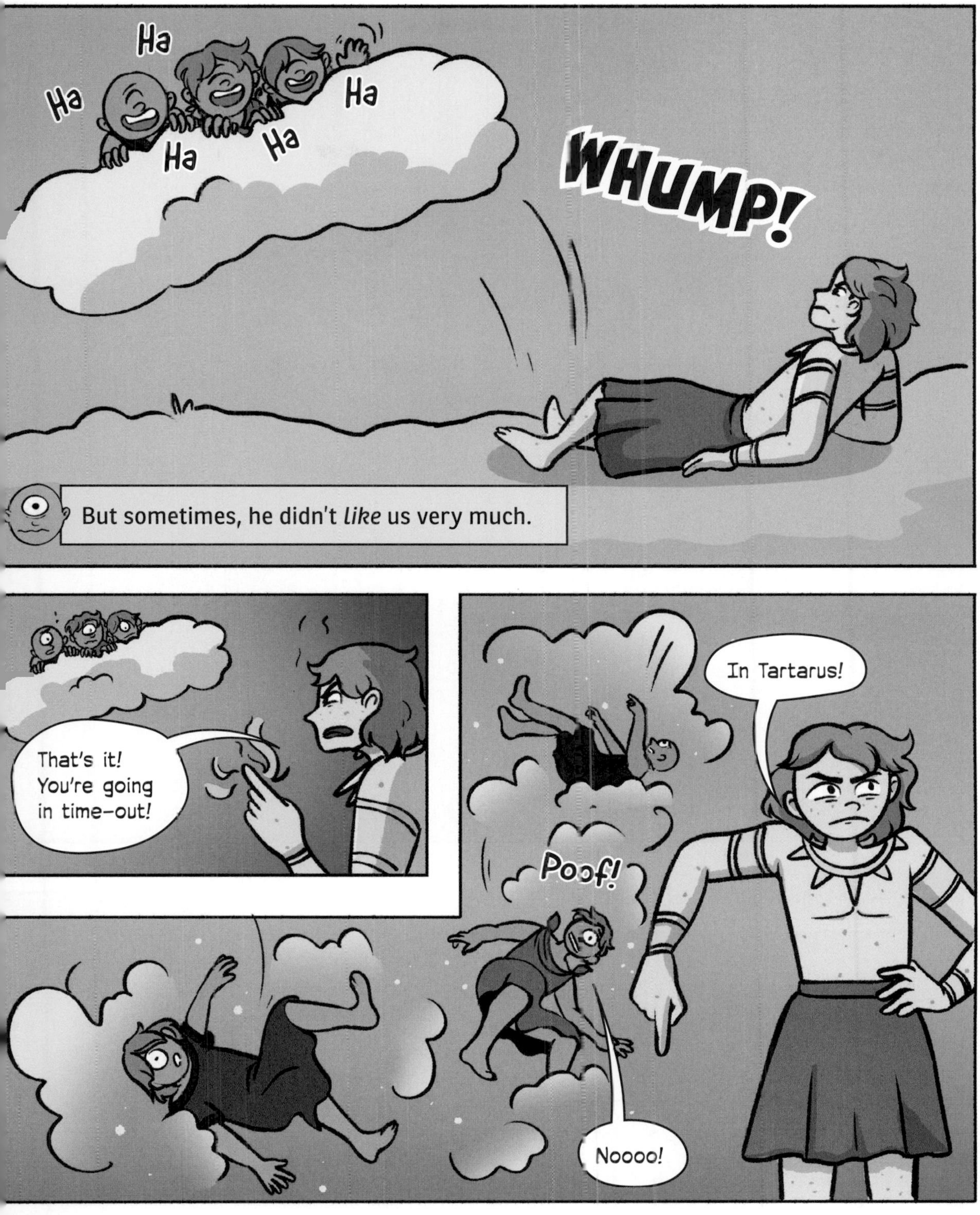
Ha
Ha
Ha
Ha
Ha
WHUMP!
But sometimes, he didn't *like* us very much.
That's it! You're going in time-out!
In Tartarus!
Poof!
Noooo!

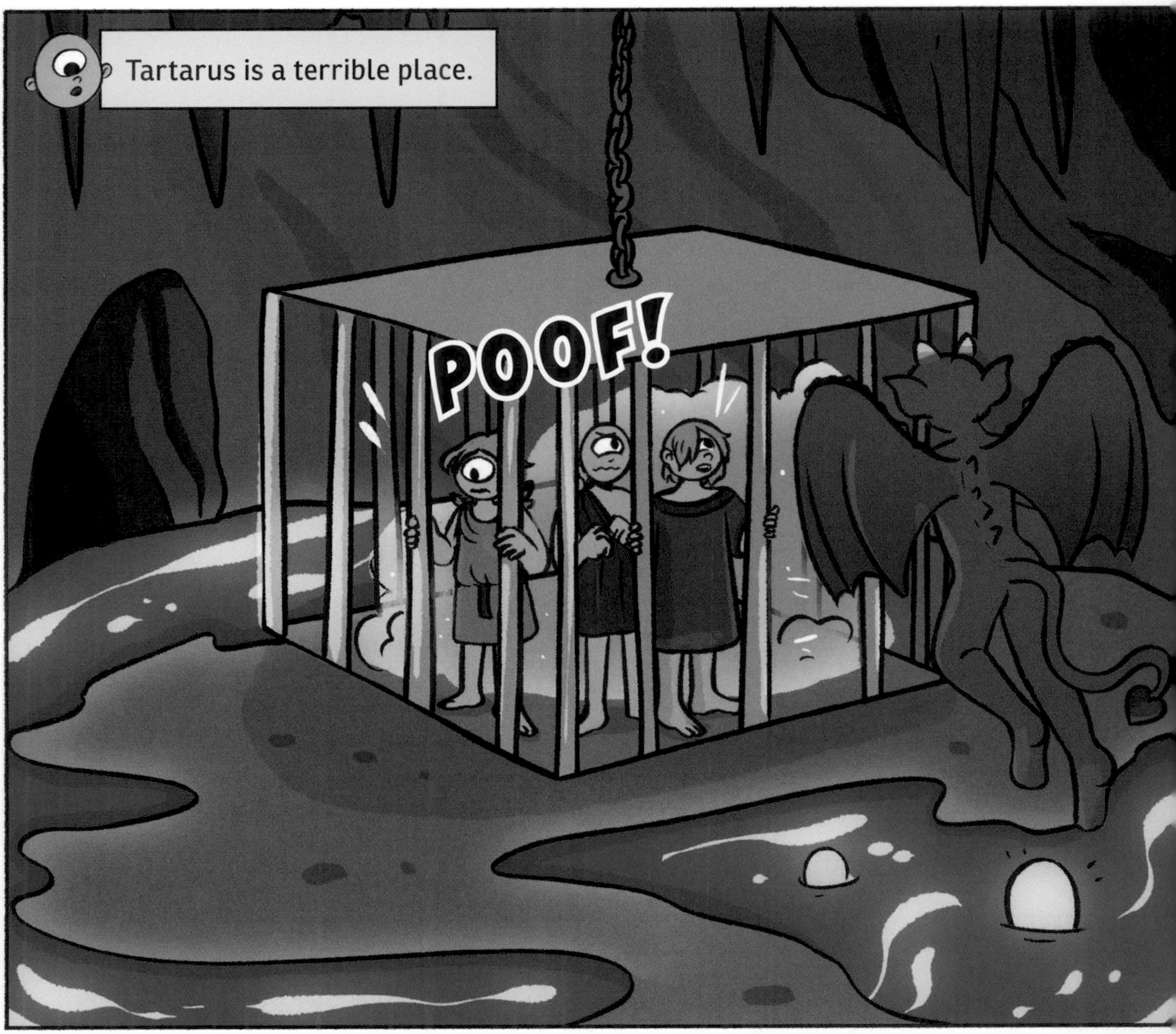
Tartarus is a terrible place.
POOF!

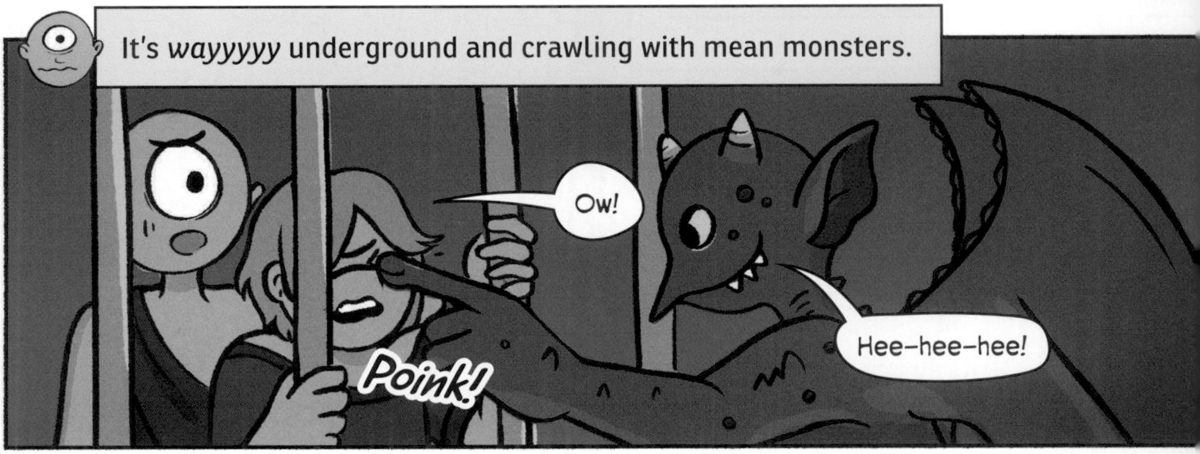
It's *wayyyyy* underground and crawling with mean monsters.
Ow!
Poink!
Hee-hee-hee!

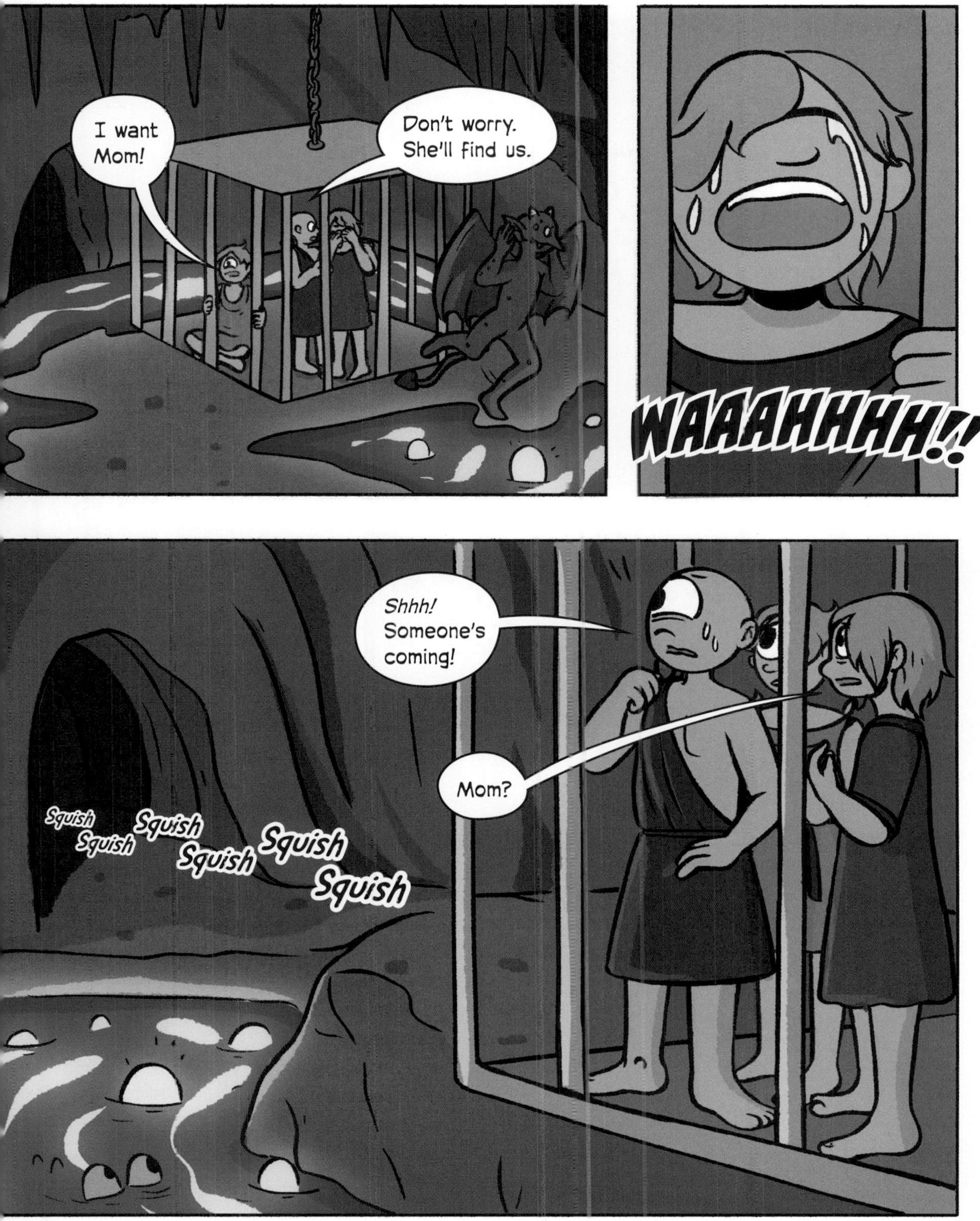
I want Mom!
Don't worry. She'll find us.
WAAAHHHH!!
Shhh! Someone's coming!
Mom?
Squish
Squish
Squish
Squish
Squish
Squish

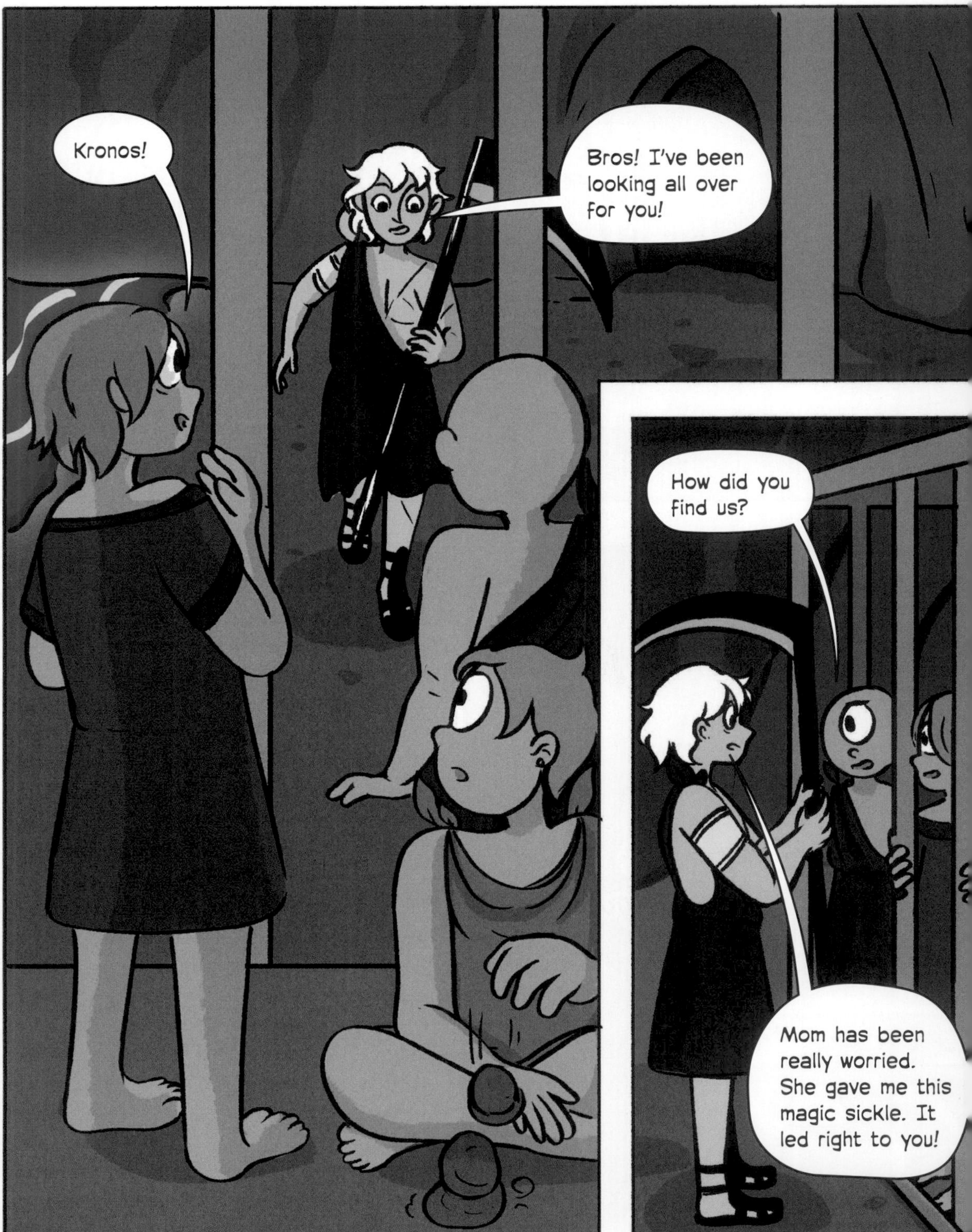
Kronos!
Bros! I've been looking all over for you!
How did you find us?
Mom has been really worried. She gave me this magic sickle. It led right to you!

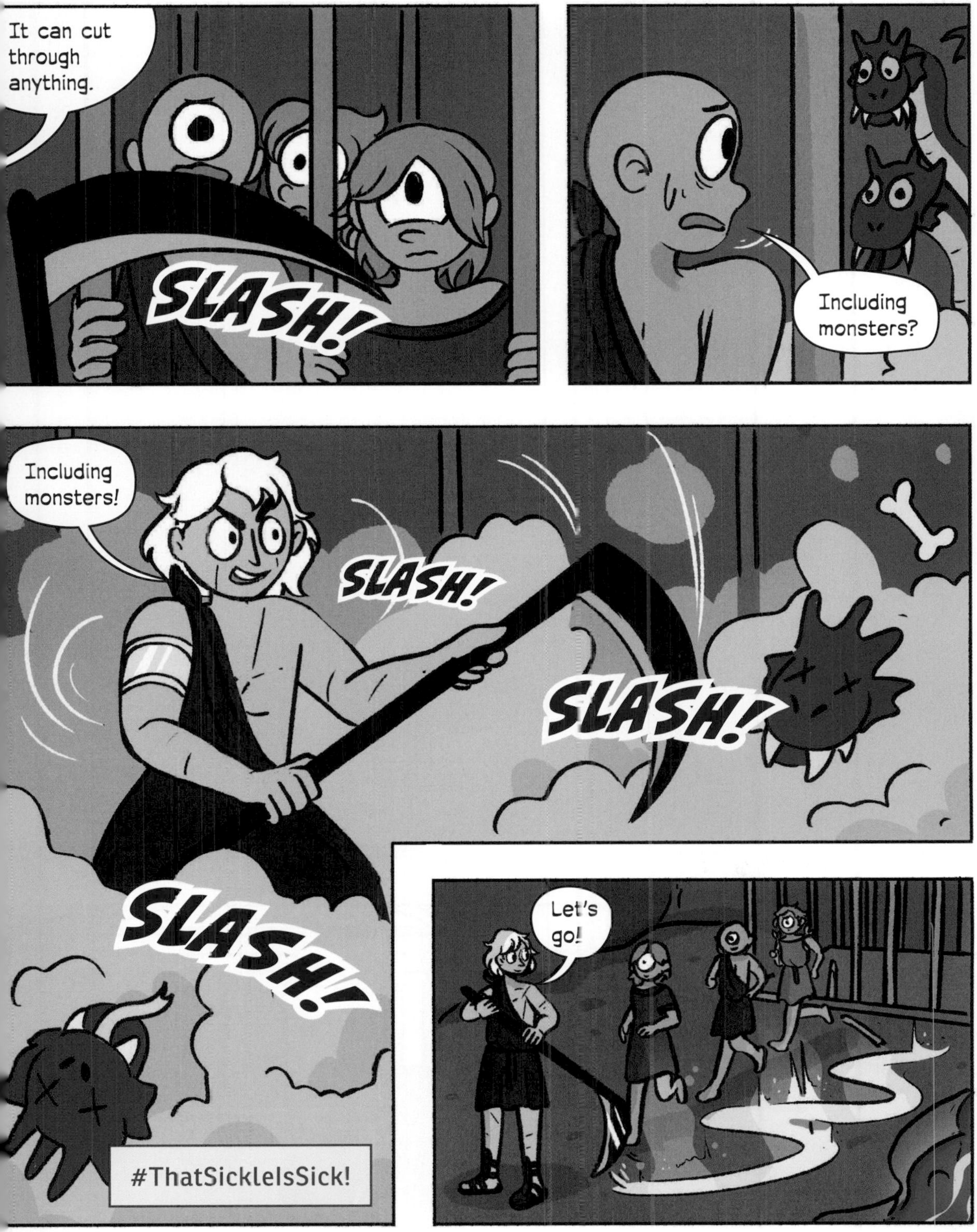
It can cut through anything.
SLASH!
Including monsters?
Including monsters!
SLASH!
SLASH!
SLASH!
#ThatSickleIsSick!
Let's go!

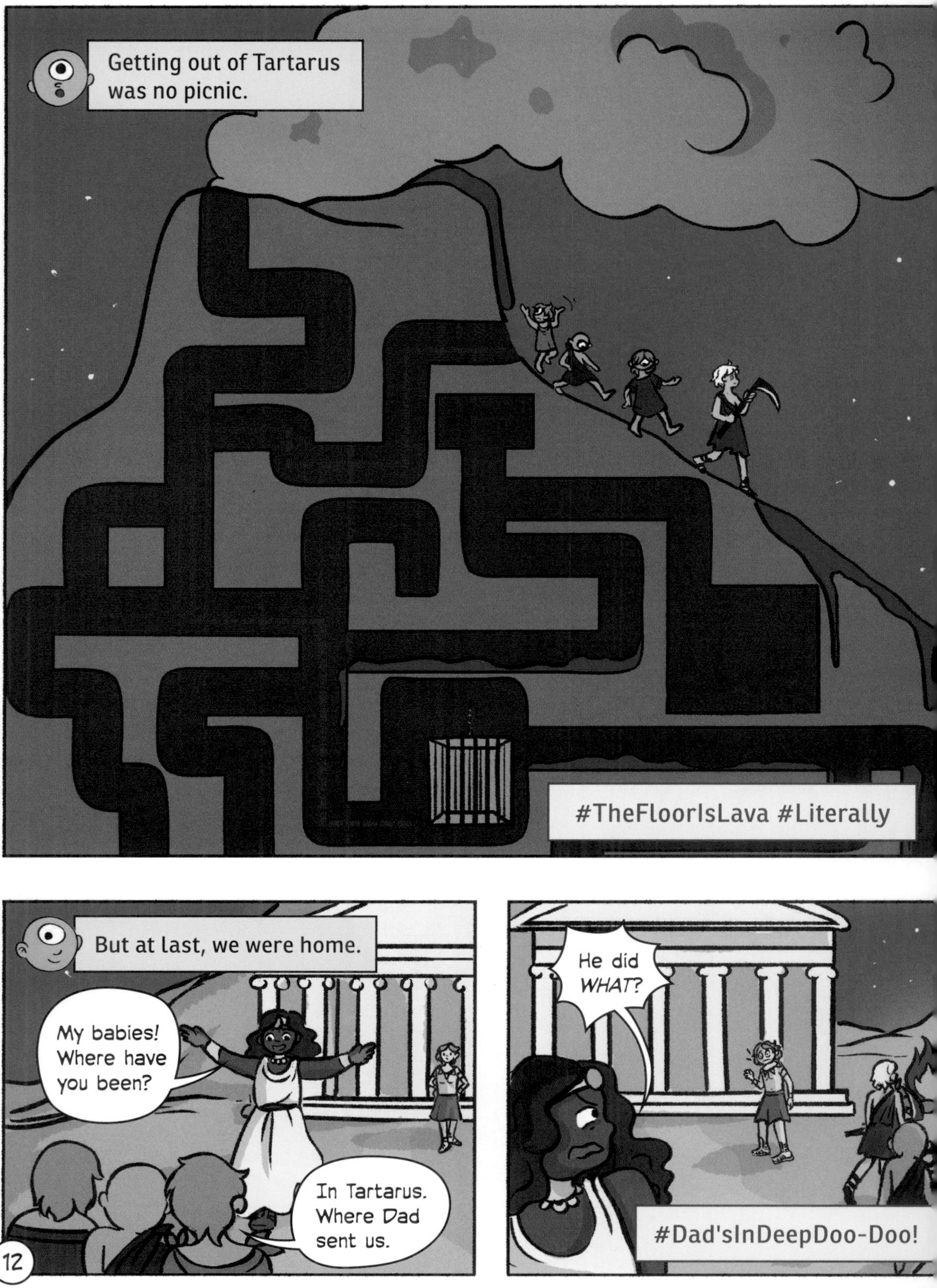
Getting out of Tartarus was no picnic.
#TheFloorIsLava #Literally
But at last, we were home.
My babies! Where have you been?
In Tartarus. Where Dad sent us.
He did *WHAT?*
#Dad'sInDeepDoo-Doo!

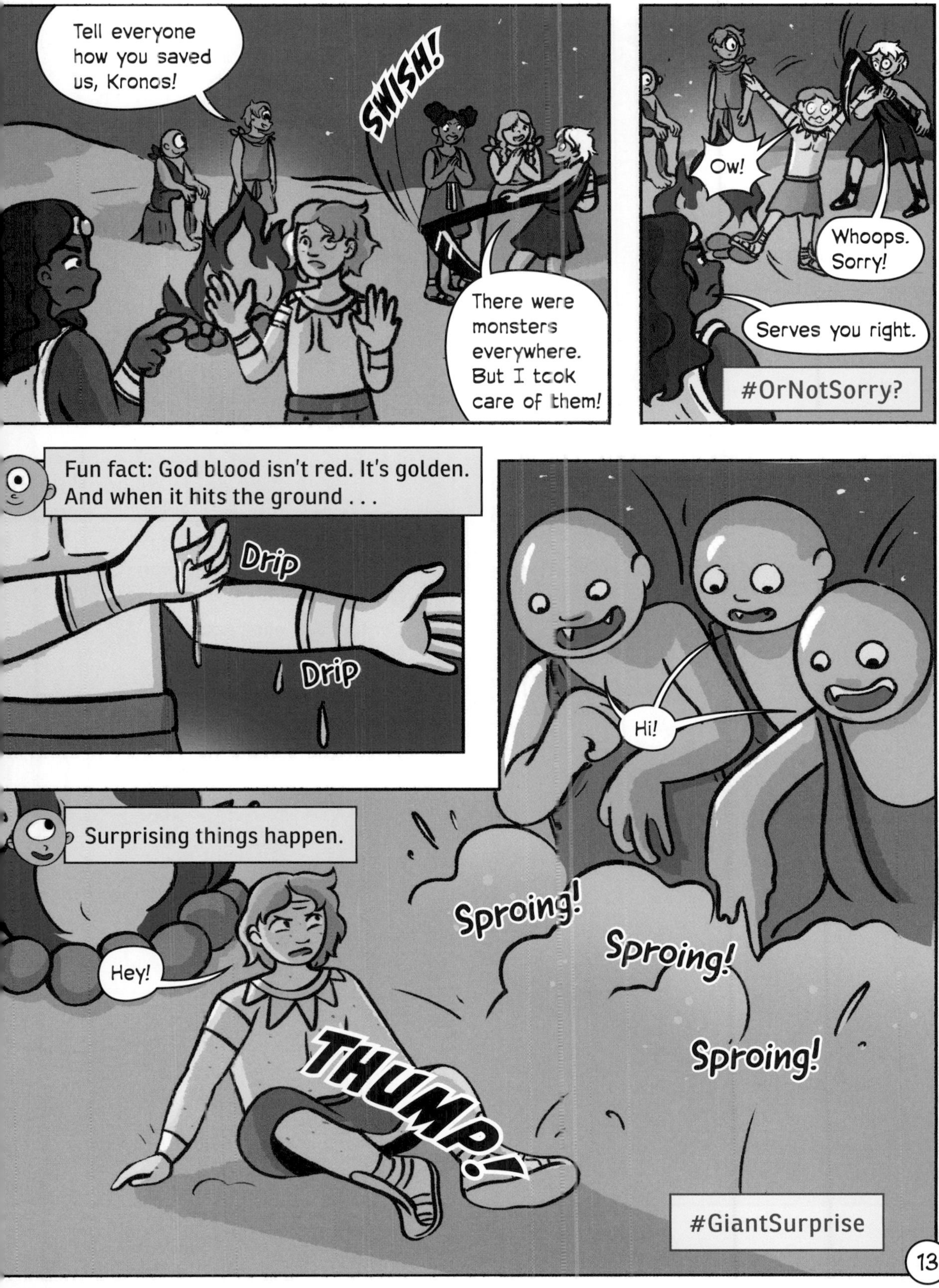
Tell everyone how you saved us, Kronos!
SWISH!
There were monsters everywhere. But I took care of them!
Ow!
Whoops. Sorry!
Serves you right.
#OrNotSorry?
Fun fact: God blood isn't red. It's golden. And when it hits the ground . . .
Drip
Drip
Hi!
Surprising things happen.
Sproing!
Sproing!
Sproing!
Hey!
THUMP!
#GiantSurprise

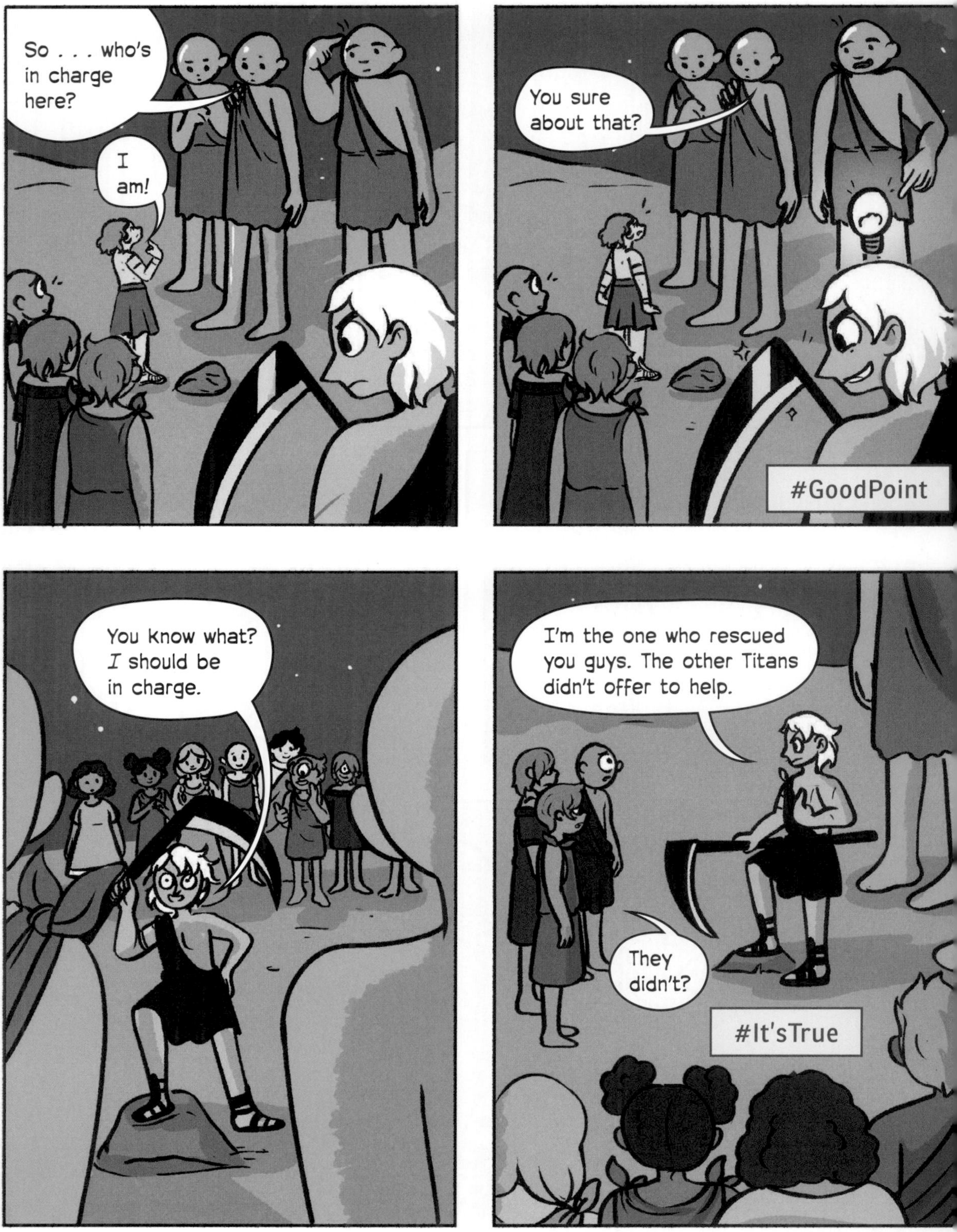
So . . . who's in charge here?
I am!
You sure about that?
#GoodPoint
You know what? *I* should be in charge.
I'm the one who rescued you guys. The other Titans didn't offer to help.
They didn't?
#It'sTrue

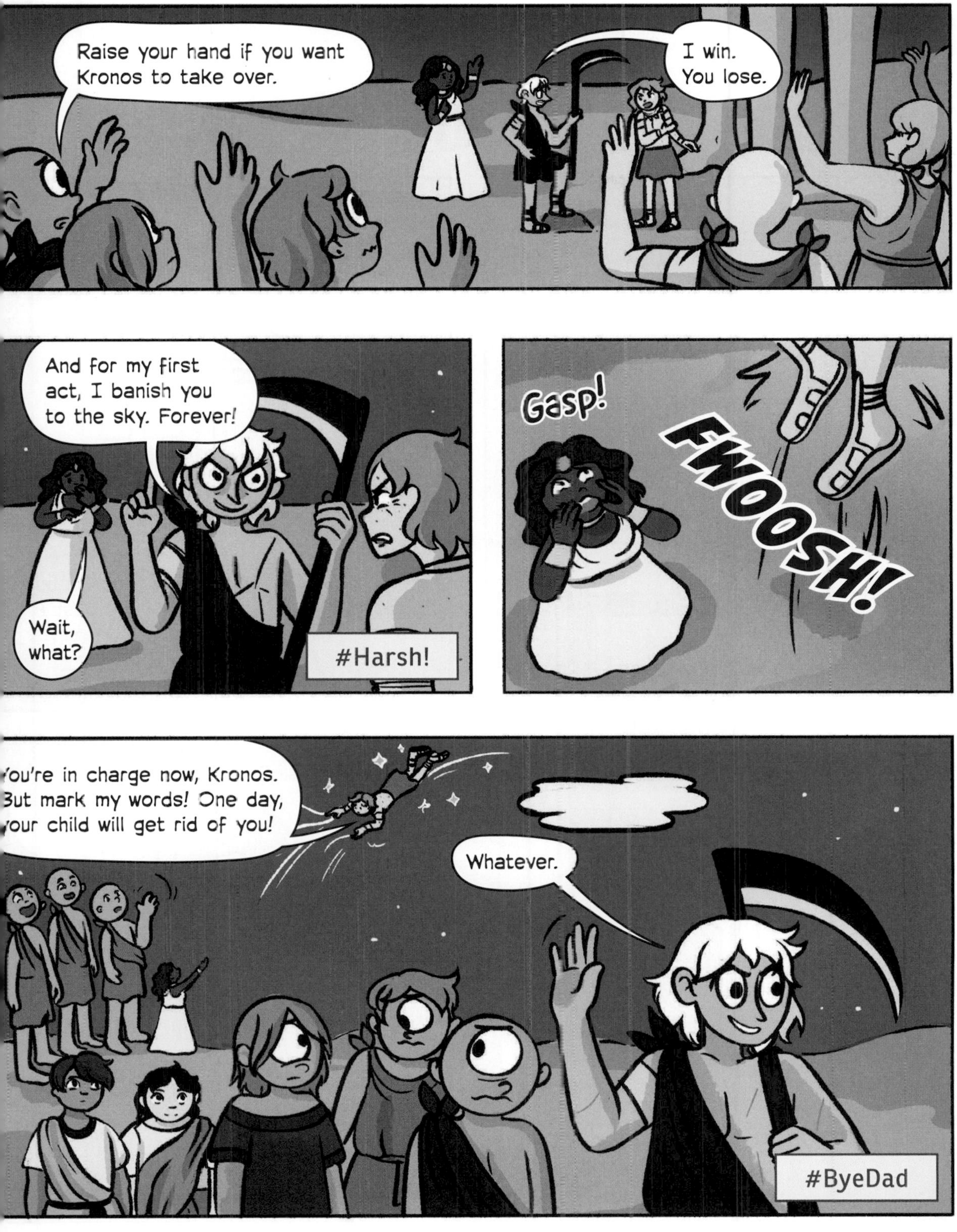
Raise your hand if you want Kronos to take over.
I win. You lose.
And for my first act, I banish you to the sky. Forever!
Wait, what?
#Harsh!
Gasp!
FWOOSH!
ou're in charge now, Kronos. But mark my words! One day, our child will get rid of you!
Whatever.
#ByeDad

CHAPTER 2

SPIT THAT OUT, KRONOS!

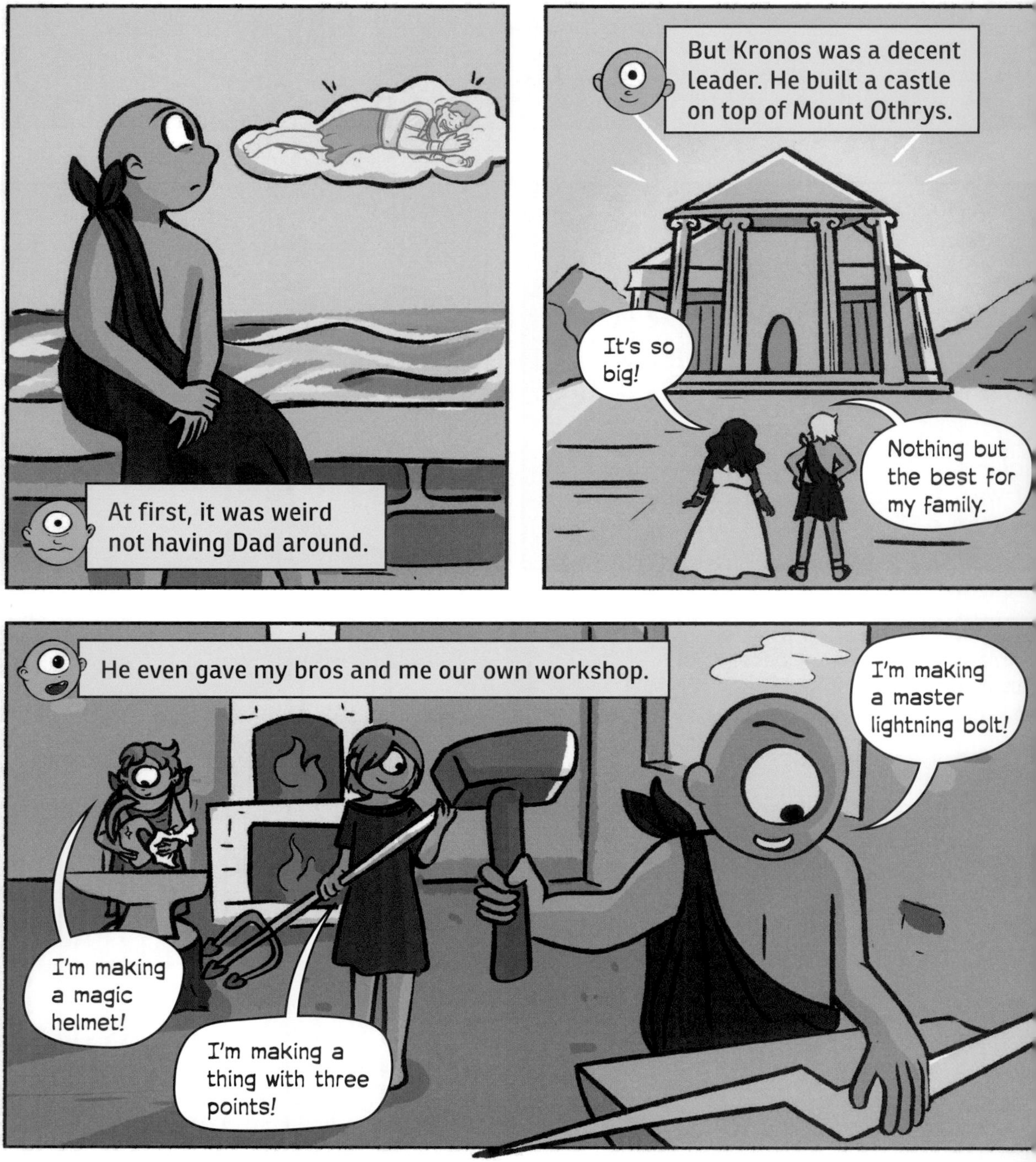

At first, it was weird not having Dad around.
But Kronos was a decent leader. He built a castle on top of Mount Othrys.
It's so big!
Nothing but the best for my family.
He even gave my bros and me our own workshop.
I'm making a master lightning bolt!
I'm making a magic helmet!
I'm making a thing with three points!

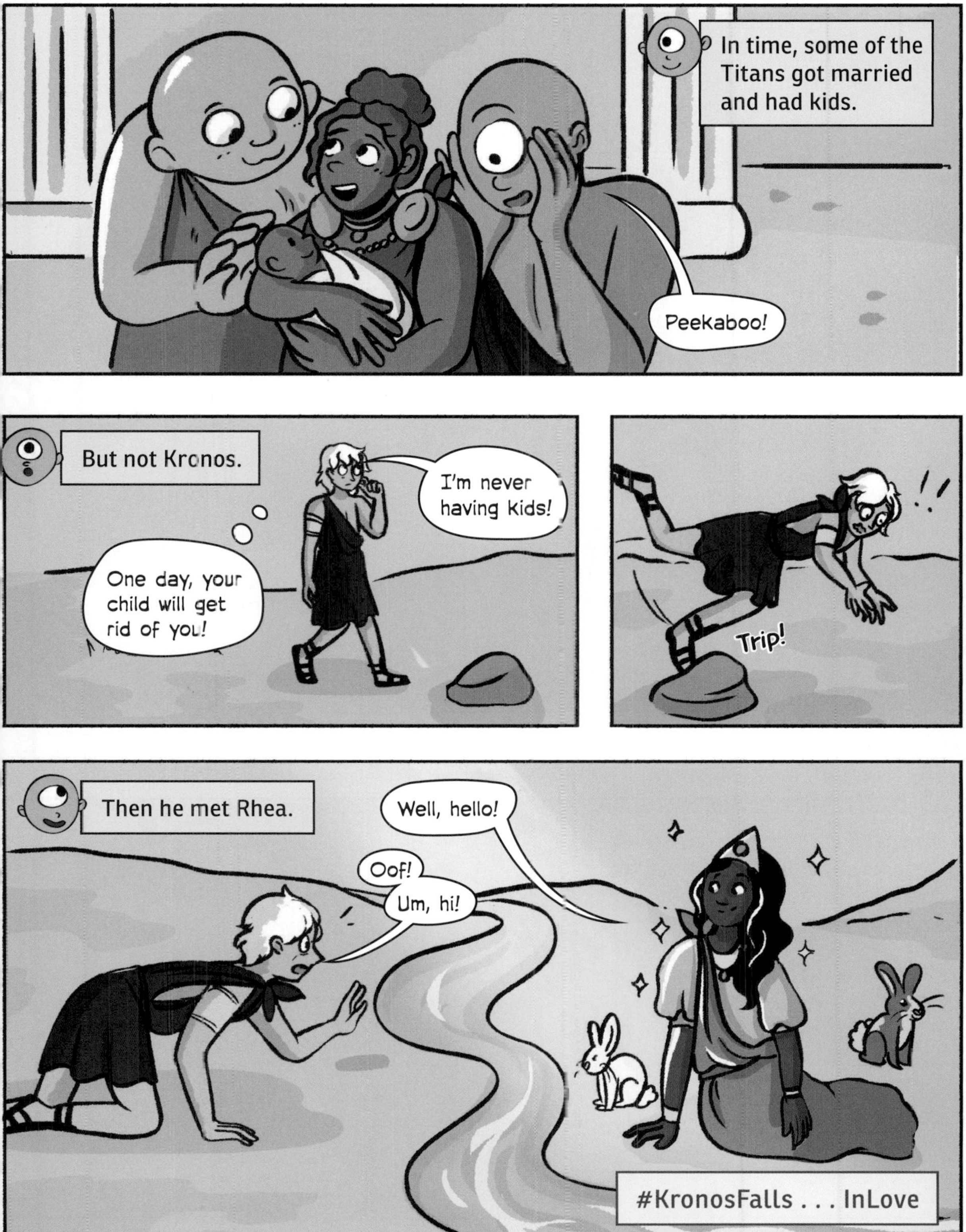
In time, some of the Titans got married and had kids.
Peekaboo!
But not Kronos.
I'm never having kids!
One day, your child will get rid of you!
Trip!
Then he met Rhea.
Well, hello!
Oof!
Um, hi!
#KronosFalls . . . InLove

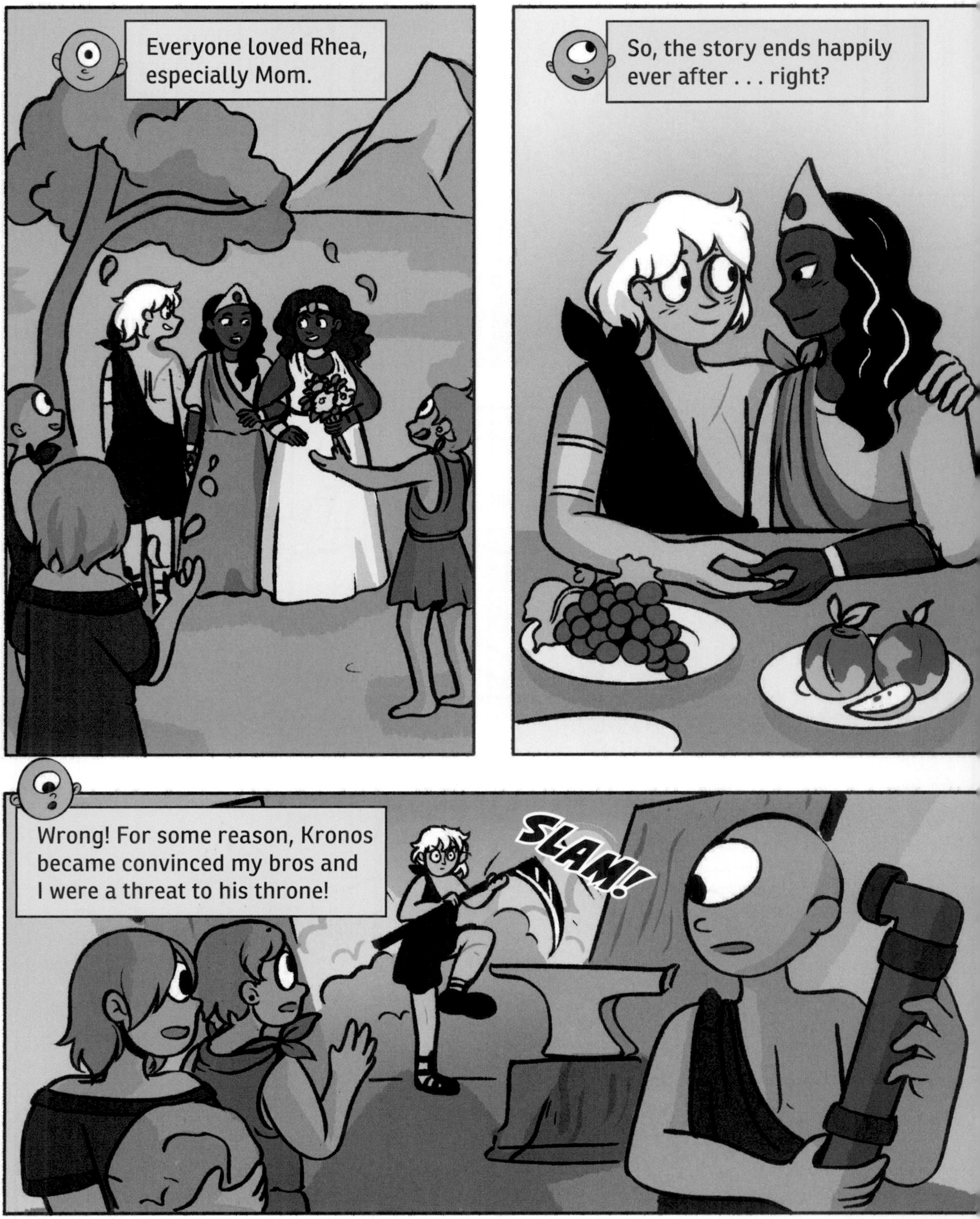
Everyone loved Rhea, especially Mom.
So, the story ends happily ever after . . . right?
Wrong! For some reason, Kronos became convinced my bros and I were a threat to his throne!
SLAM!

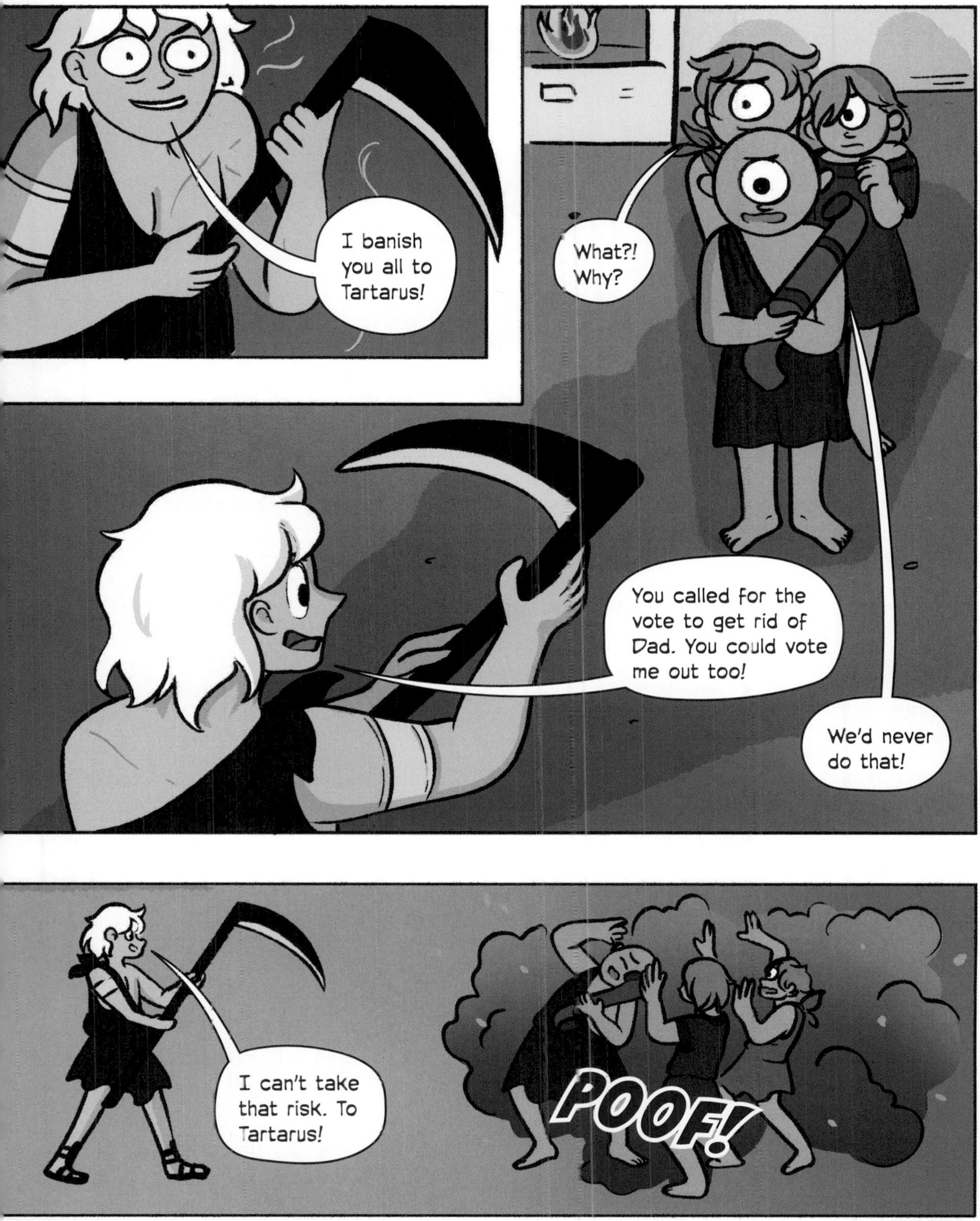
I banish you all to Tartarus!
What?! Why?
You called for the vote to get rid of Dad. You could vote me out too!
We'd never do that!
I can't take that risk. To Tartarus!
POOF!

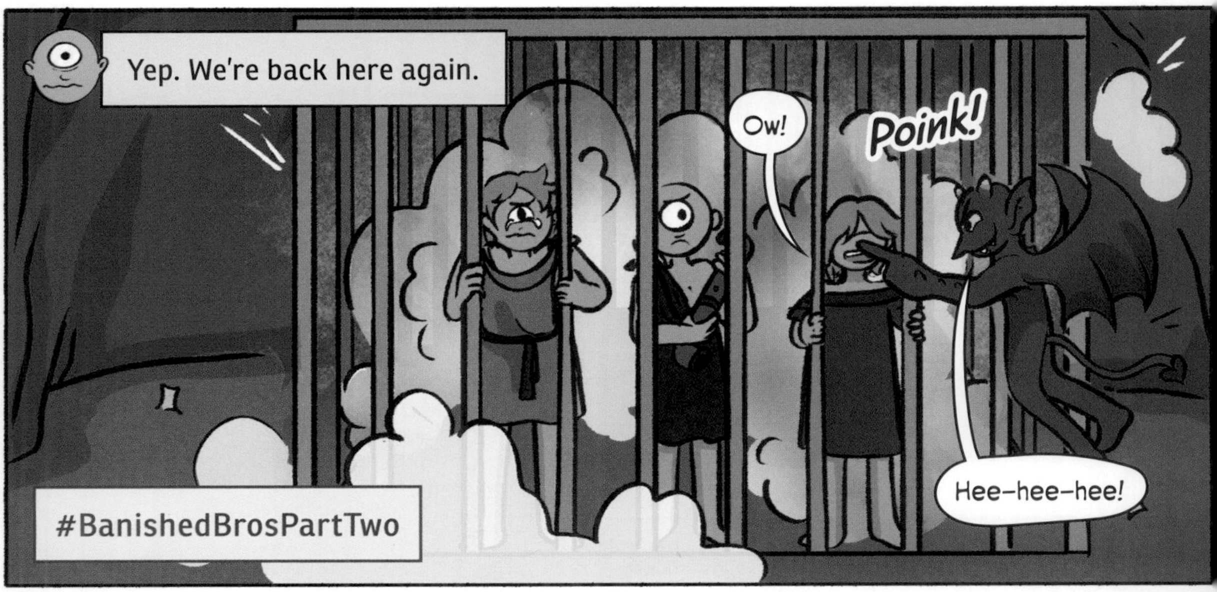
Yep. We're back here again.
Ow!
Poink!
Hee-hee-hee!
#BanishedBrosPartTwo

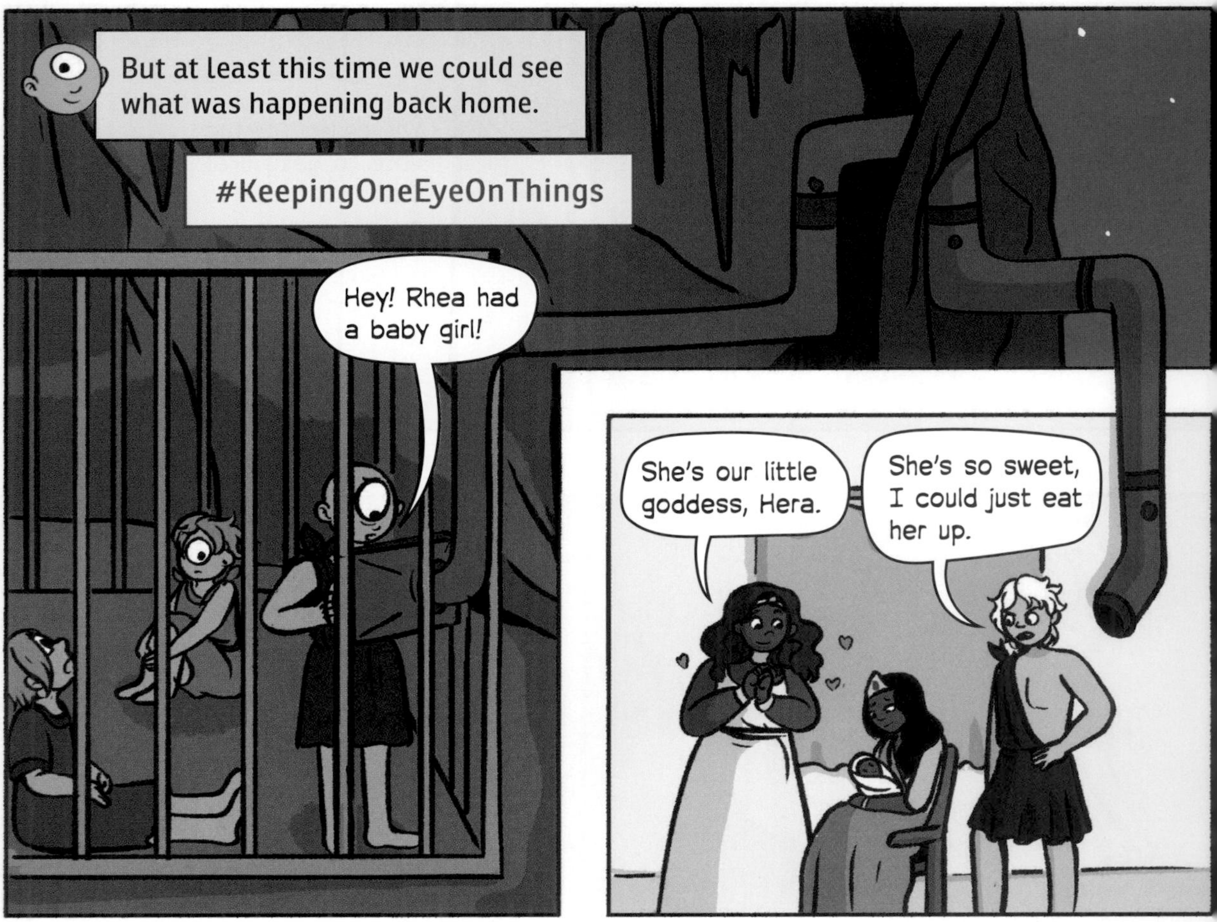
But at least this time we could see what was happening back home.
#KeepingOneEyeOnThings
Hey! Rhea had a baby girl!
She's our little goddess, Hera.
She's so sweet, I could just eat her up.

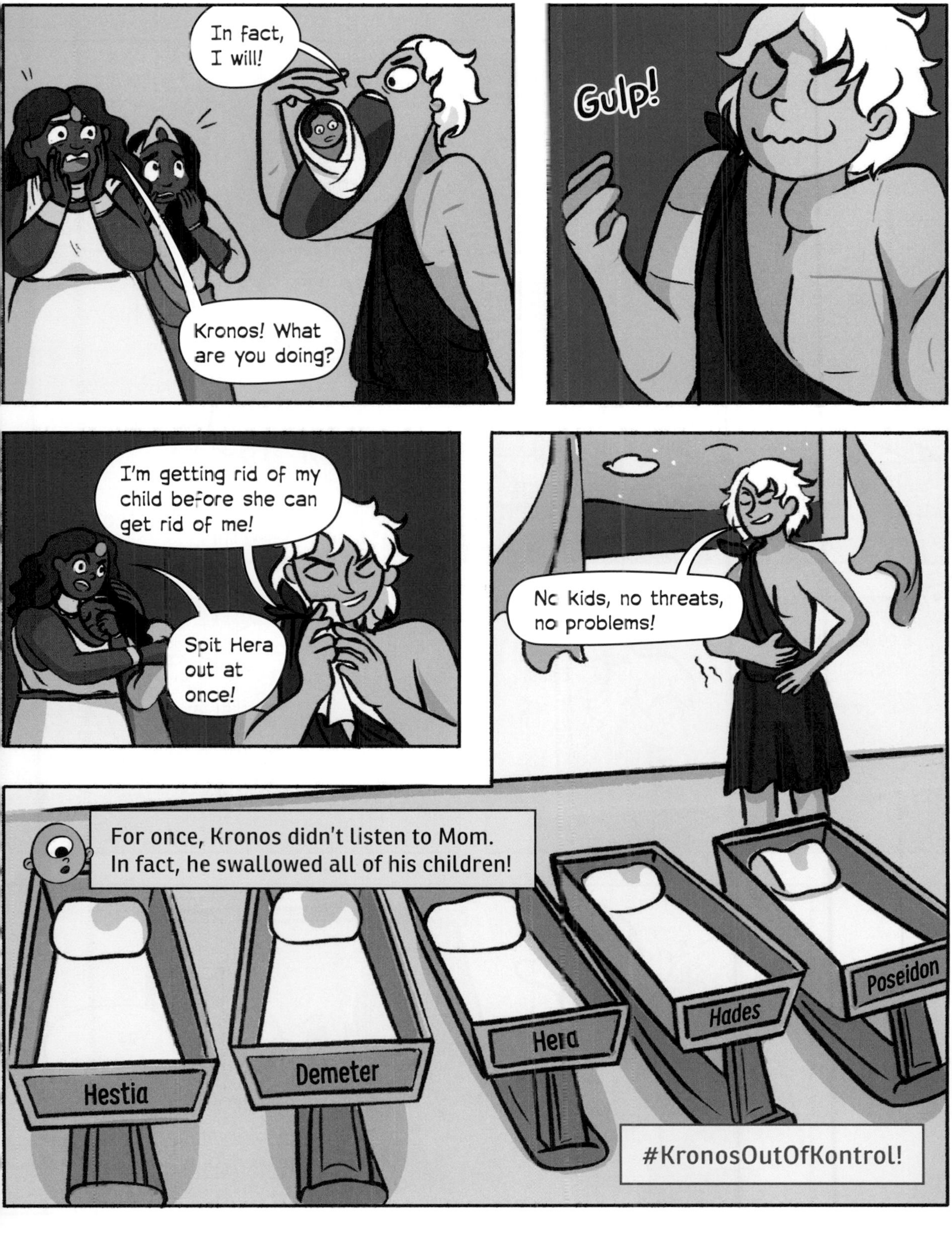
In fact, I will!
Kronos! What are you doing?
Gulp!
I'm getting rid of my child before she can get rid of me!
Spit Hera out at once!
No kids, no threats, no problems!
For once, Kronos didn't listen to Mom. In fact, he swallowed all of his children!
Hestia
Demeter
Hera
Hades
Poseidon
#KronosOutOfKontrol!

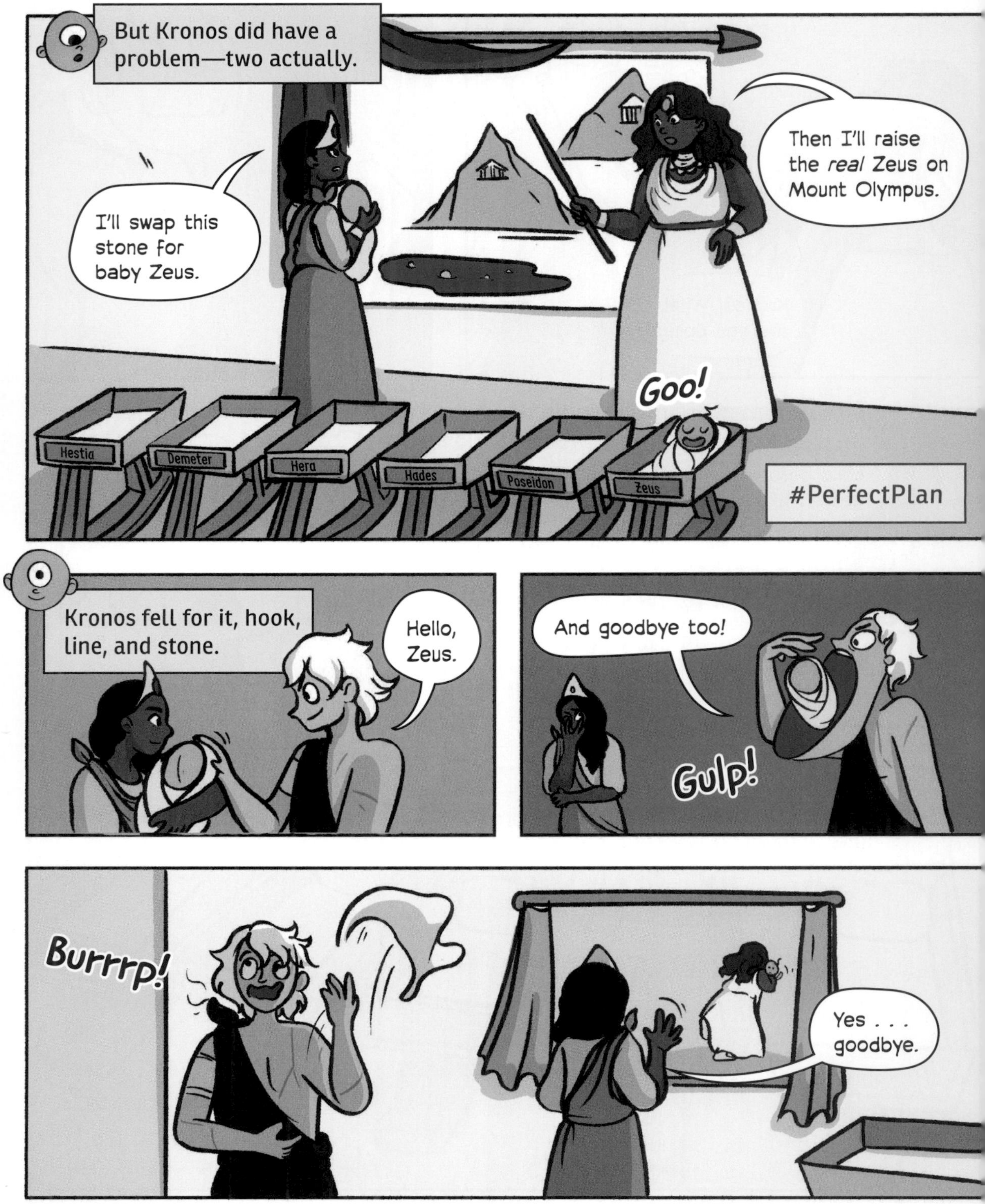
But Kronos did have a problem—two actually.
I'll swap this stone for baby Zeus.
Then I'll raise the *real* Zeus on Mount Olympus.
Goo!
Hestia
Demeter
Hera
Hades
Poseidon
Zeus
#PerfectPlan
Kronos fell for it, hook, line, and stone.
Hello, Zeus.
And goodbye too!
Gulp!
Burrrp!
Yes . . . goodbye.

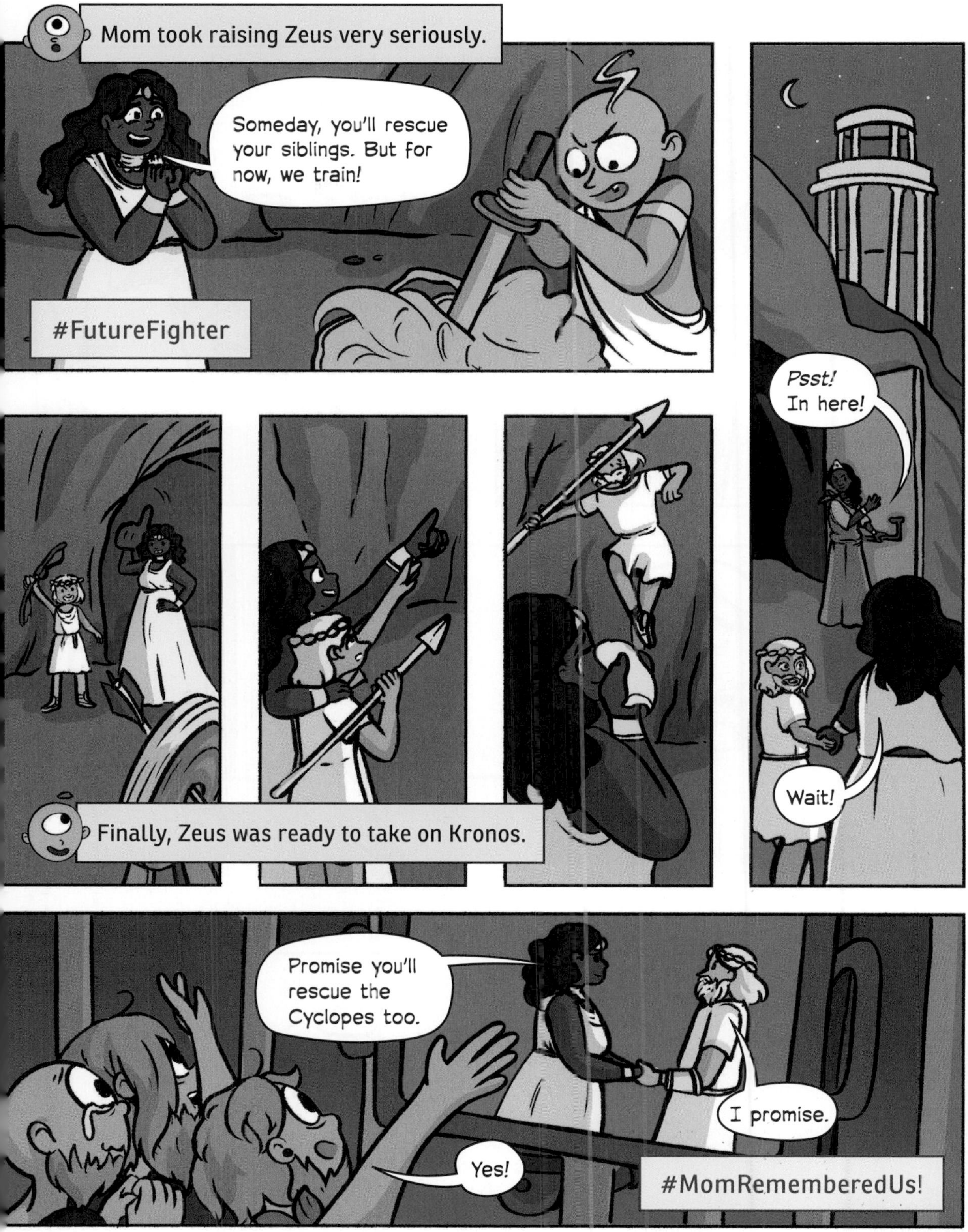
Mom took raising Zeus very seriously.
Someday, you'll rescue your siblings. But for now, we train!
#FutureFighter
Psst! In here!
Wait!
Finally, Zeus was ready to take on Kronos.
Promise you'll rescue the Cyclopes too.
I promise.
Yes!
#MomRememberedUs!

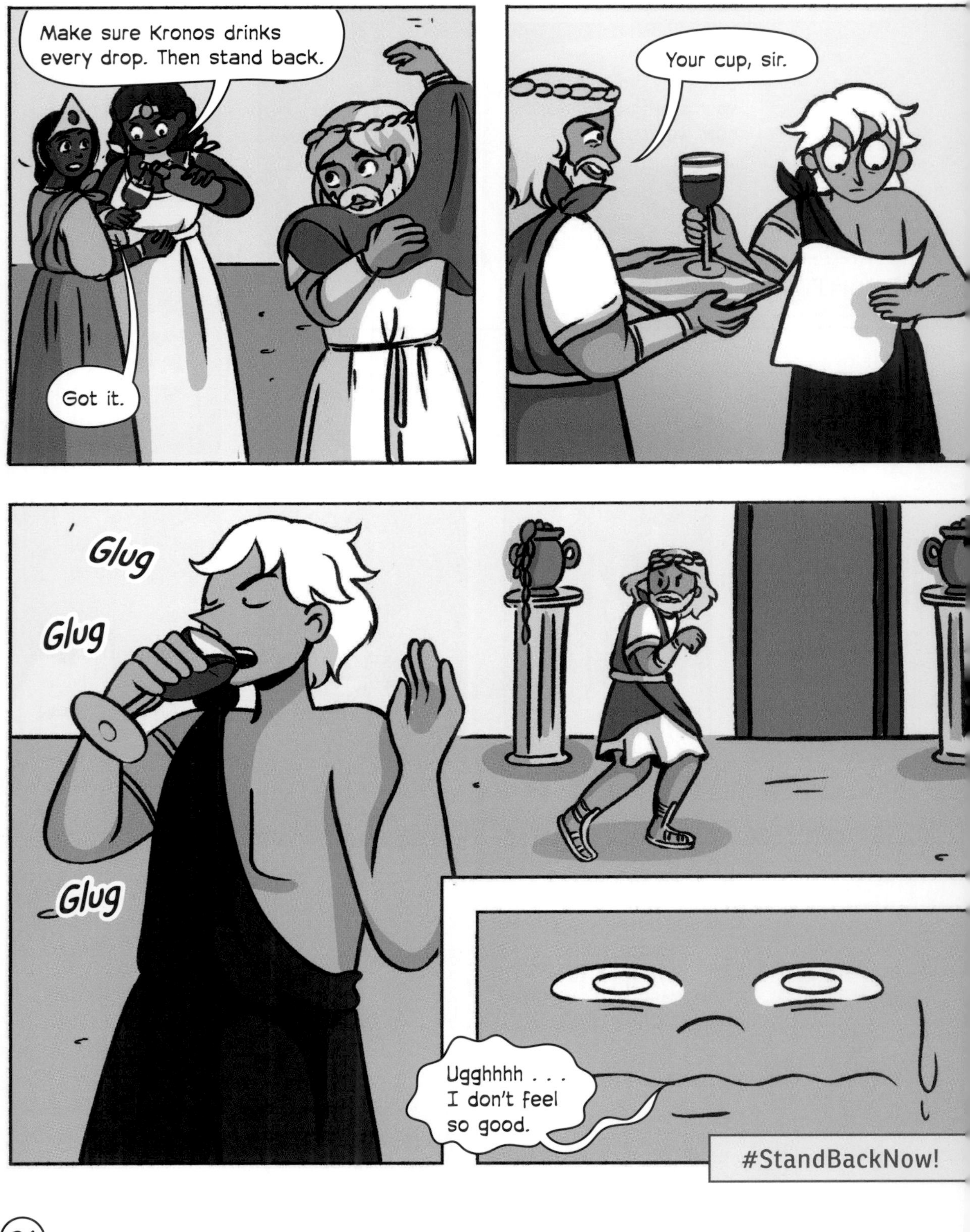
Make sure Kronos drinks every drop. Then stand back.
Got it.
Your cup, sir.
Glug
Glug
Glug
Ugghhhh . . . I don't feel so good.
#StandBackNow!

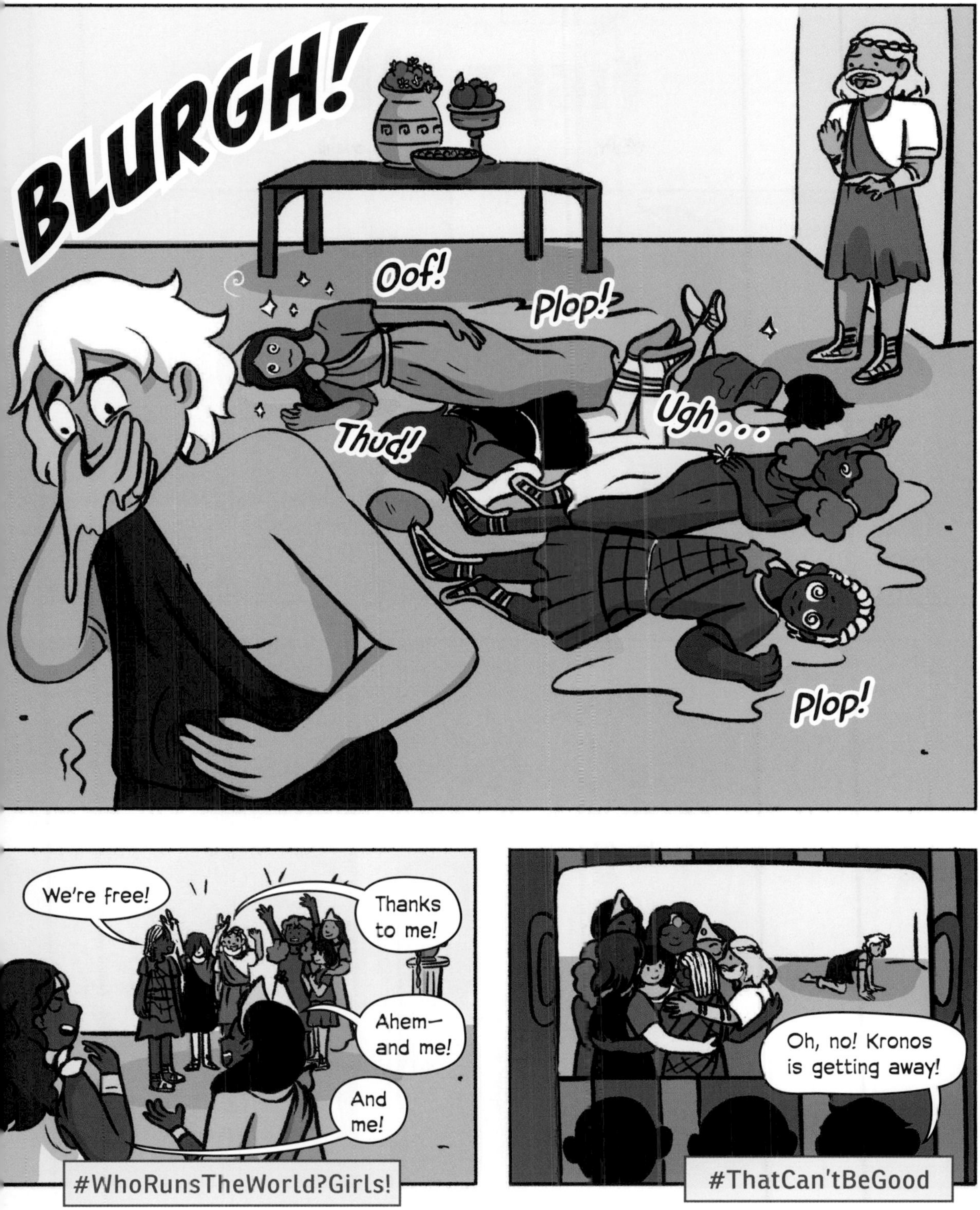
BLURGH!
Oof!
Plop!
Thud!
Ugh . . .
Plop!
We're free!
Thanks to me!
Ahem—and me!
And me!
#WhoRunsTheWorld?Girls!
Oh, no! Kronos is getting away!
#ThatCan'tBeGood

CHAPTER 3

FIGHT ME!

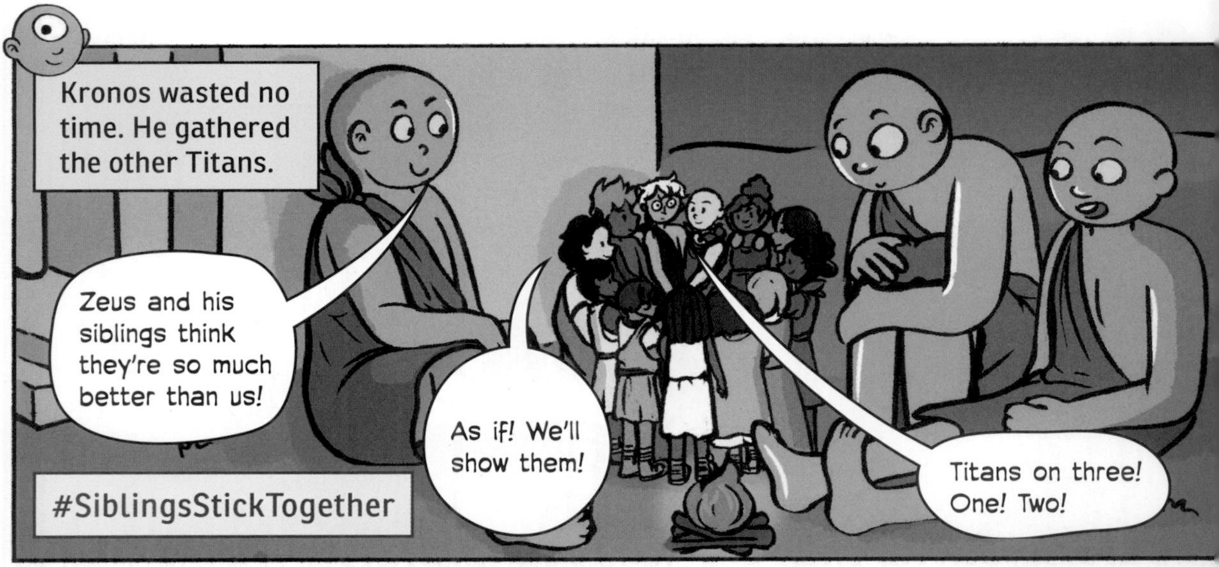
Kronos wasted no time. He gathered the other Titans.
Zeus and his siblings think they're so much better than us!
As if! We'll show them!
Titans on three! One! Two!
#SiblingsStickTogether

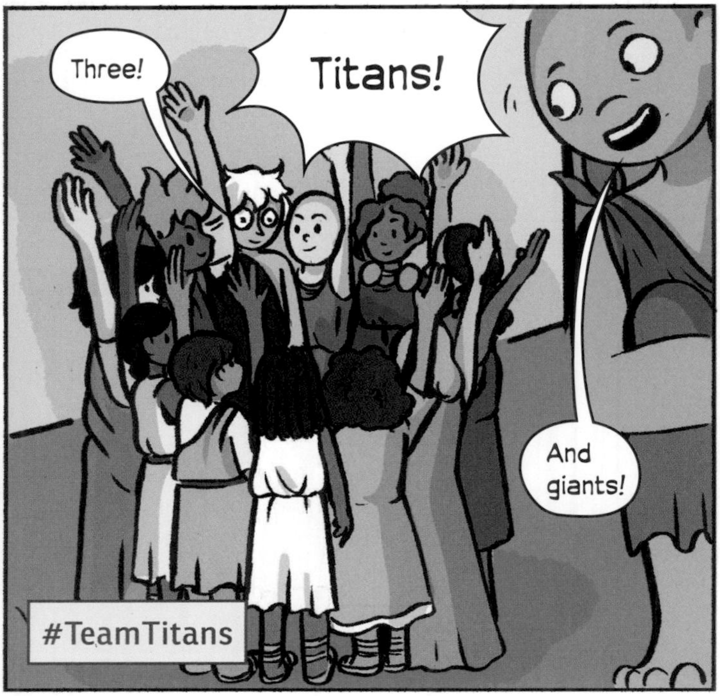
Three!
Titans!
And giants!
#TeamTitans

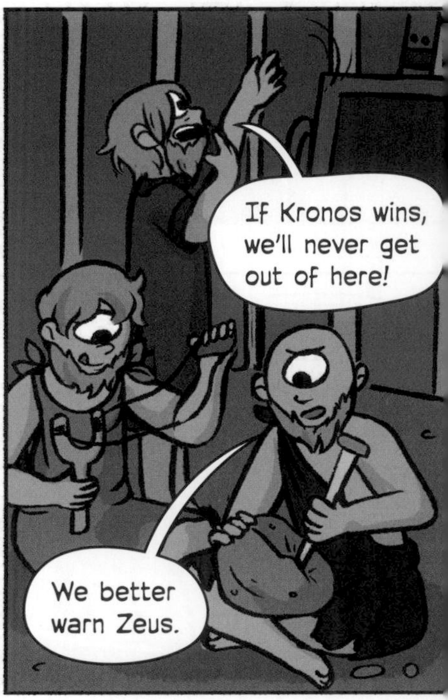
If Kronos wins, we'll never get out of here!
We better warn Zeus.

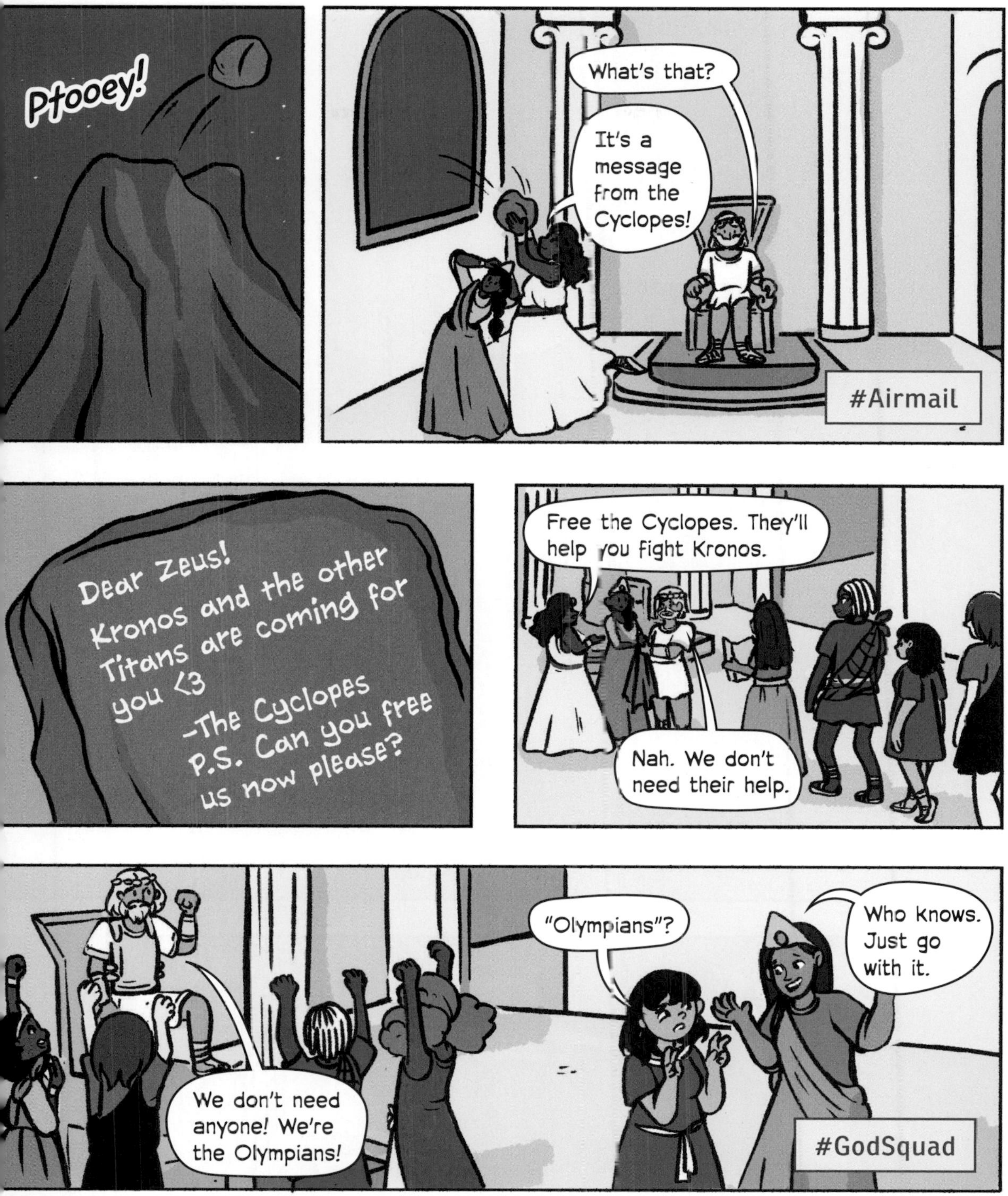
Ptooey!
What's that?
It's a message from the Cyclopes!
#Airmail
Dear Zeus!
Kronos and the other Titans are coming for you <3
-The Cyclopes
P.S. Can you free us now please?
Free the Cyclopes. They'll help you fight Kronos.
Nah. We don't need their help.
We don't need anyone! We're the Olympians!
"Olympians"?
Who knows. Just go with it.
#GodSquad

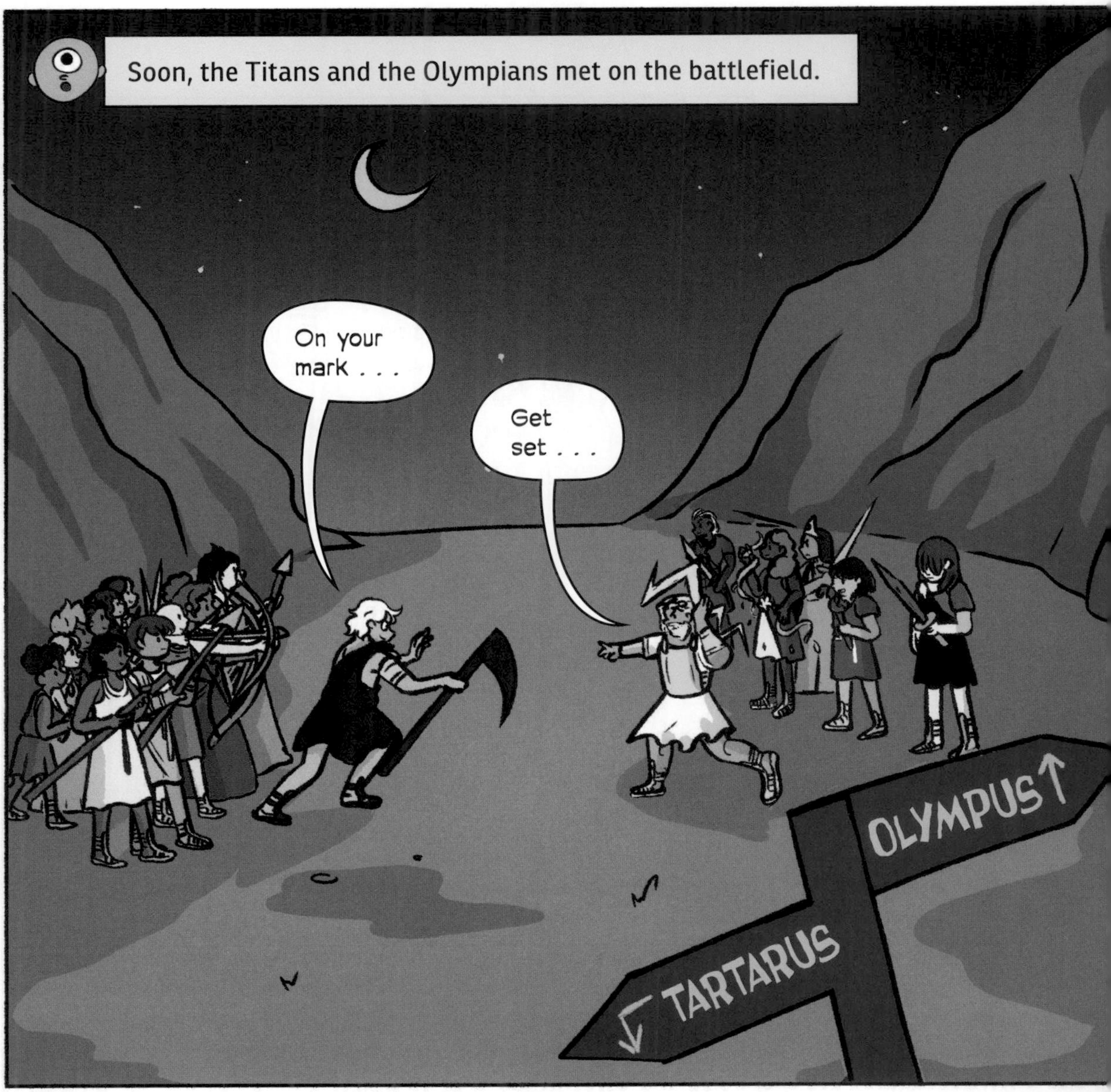
Soon, the Titans and the Olympians met on the battlefield.
On your mark . . .
Get set . . .
OLYMPUS
TARTARUS

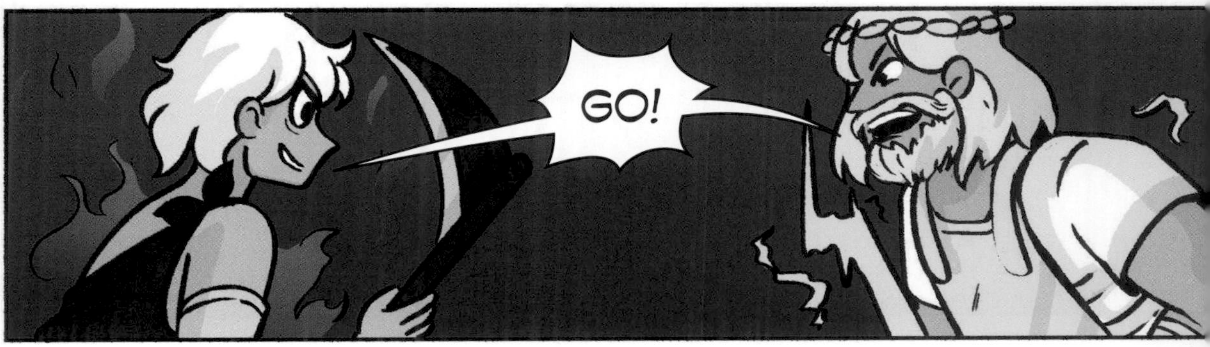
GO!

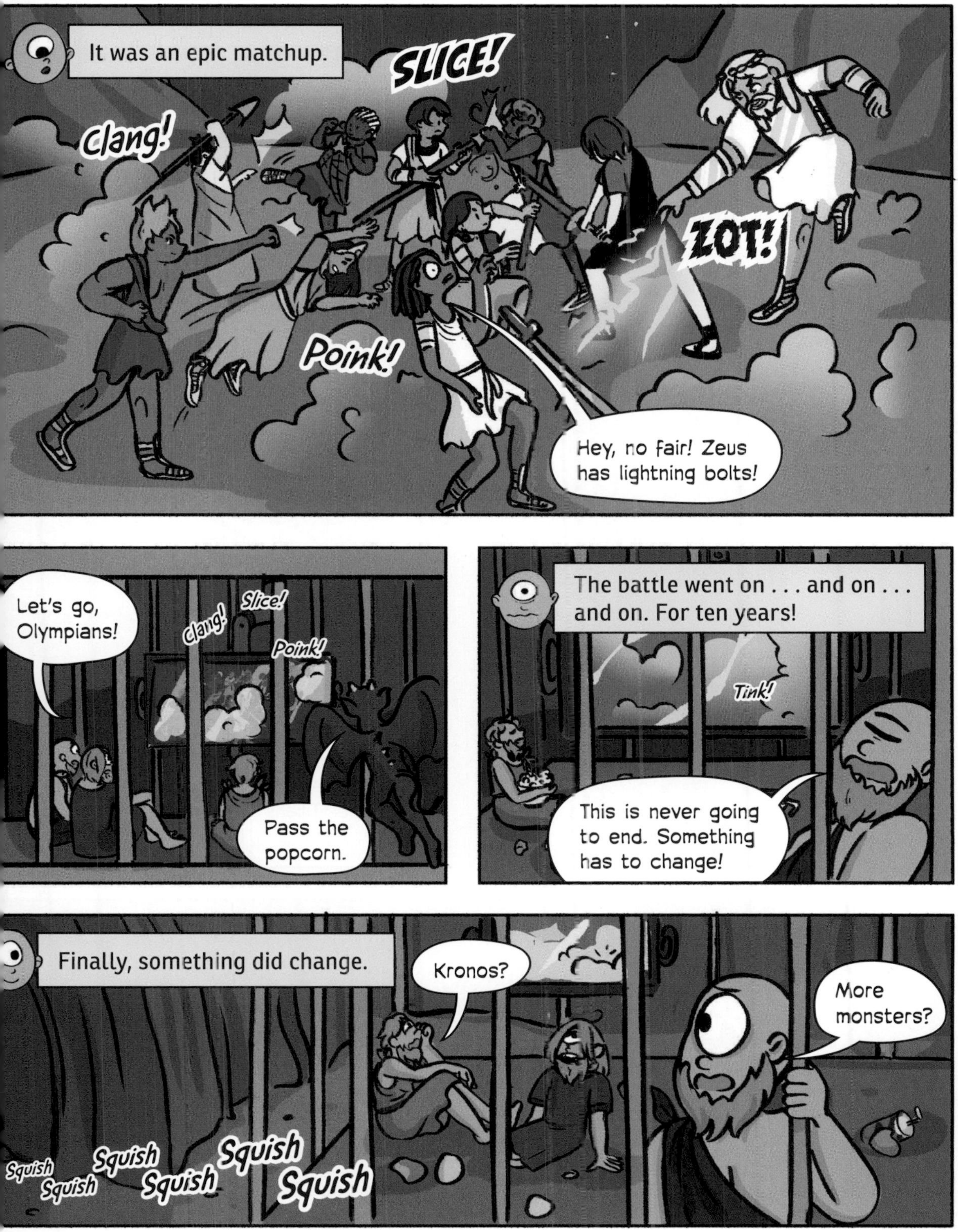
It was an epic matchup.
SLICE!
Clang!
ZOT!
Poink!
Hey, no fair! Zeus has lightning bolts!
Let's go, Olympians!
Clang!
Slice!
Poink!
Pass the popcorn.
The battle went on . . . and on . . . and on. For ten years!
Tink!
This is never going to end. Something has to change!
Finally, something did change.
Kronos?
More monsters?
Squish
Squish
Squish
Squish
Squish
Squish

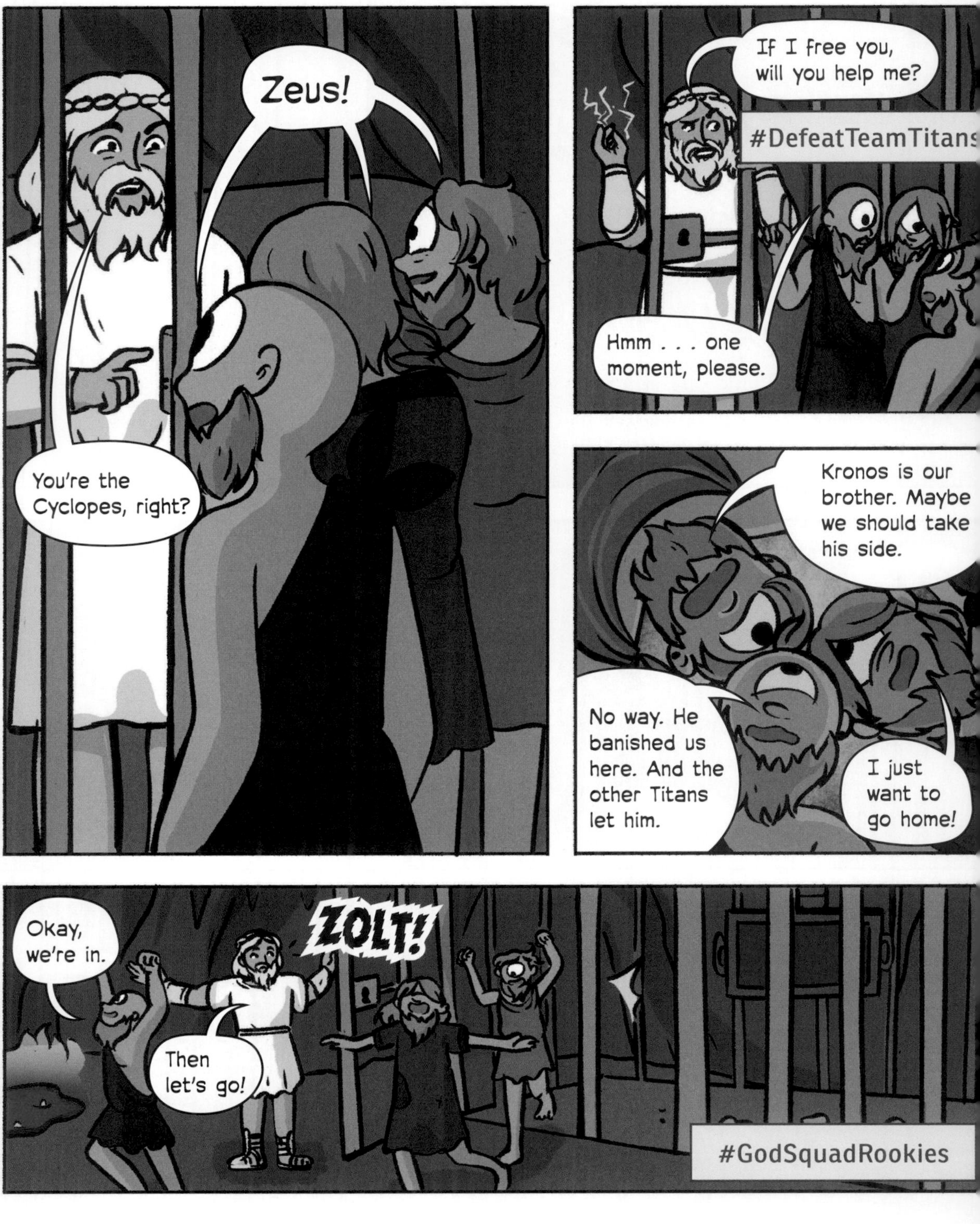
Zeus!
You're the Cyclopes, right?
If I free you, will you help me?
#DefeatTeamTitans
Hmm . . . one moment, please.
Kronos is our brother. Maybe we should take his side.
No way. He banished us here. And the other Titans let him.
I just want to go home!
Okay, we're in.
ZOLT!
Then let's go!
#GodSquadRookies

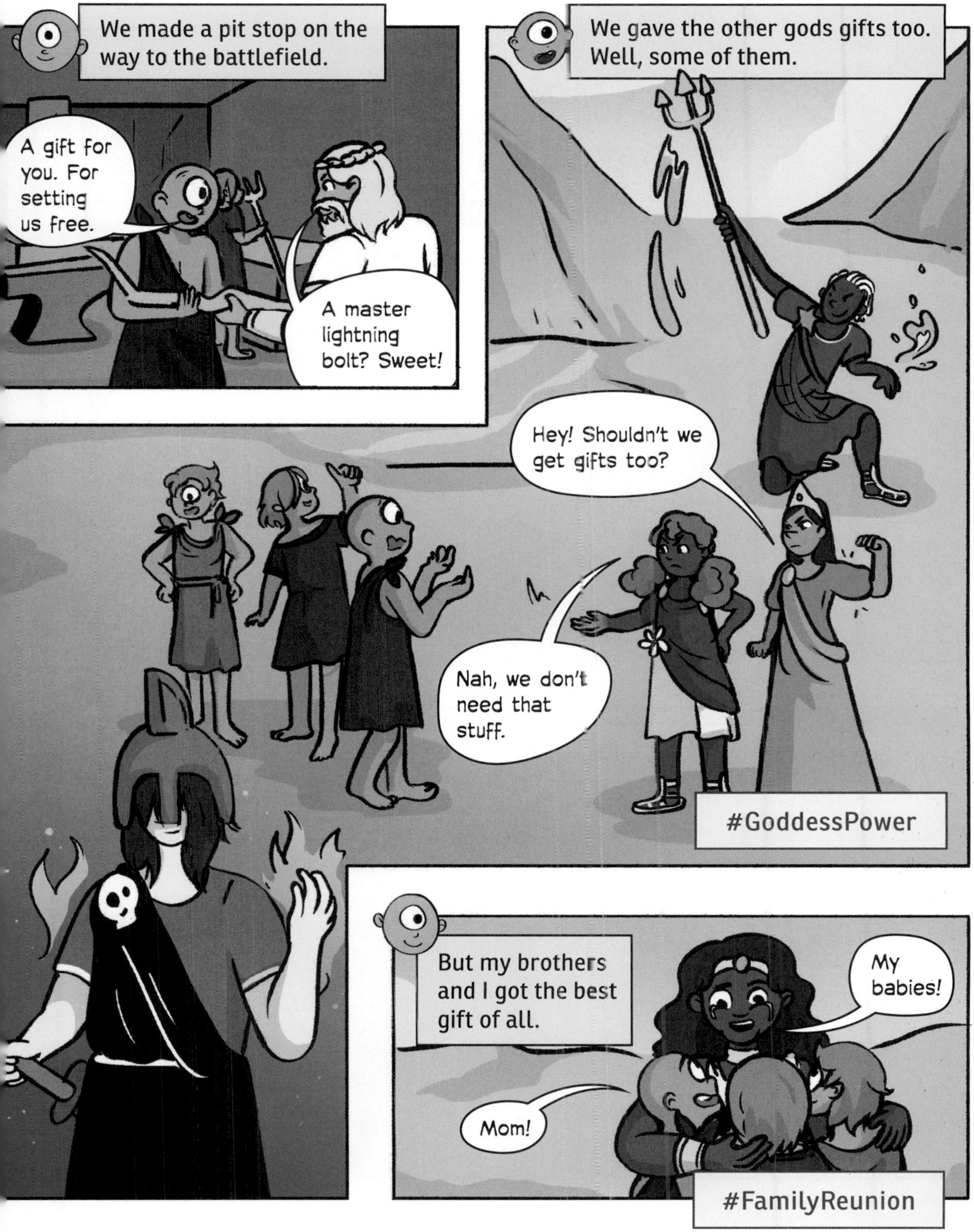

We made a pit stop on the way to the battlefield.
A gift for you. For setting us free.
A master lightning bolt? Sweet!
We gave the other gods gifts too. Well, some of them.
Hey! Shouldn't we get gifts too?
Nah, we don't need that stuff.
#GoddessPower
But my brothers and I got the best gift of all.
My babies!
Mom!
#FamilyReunion

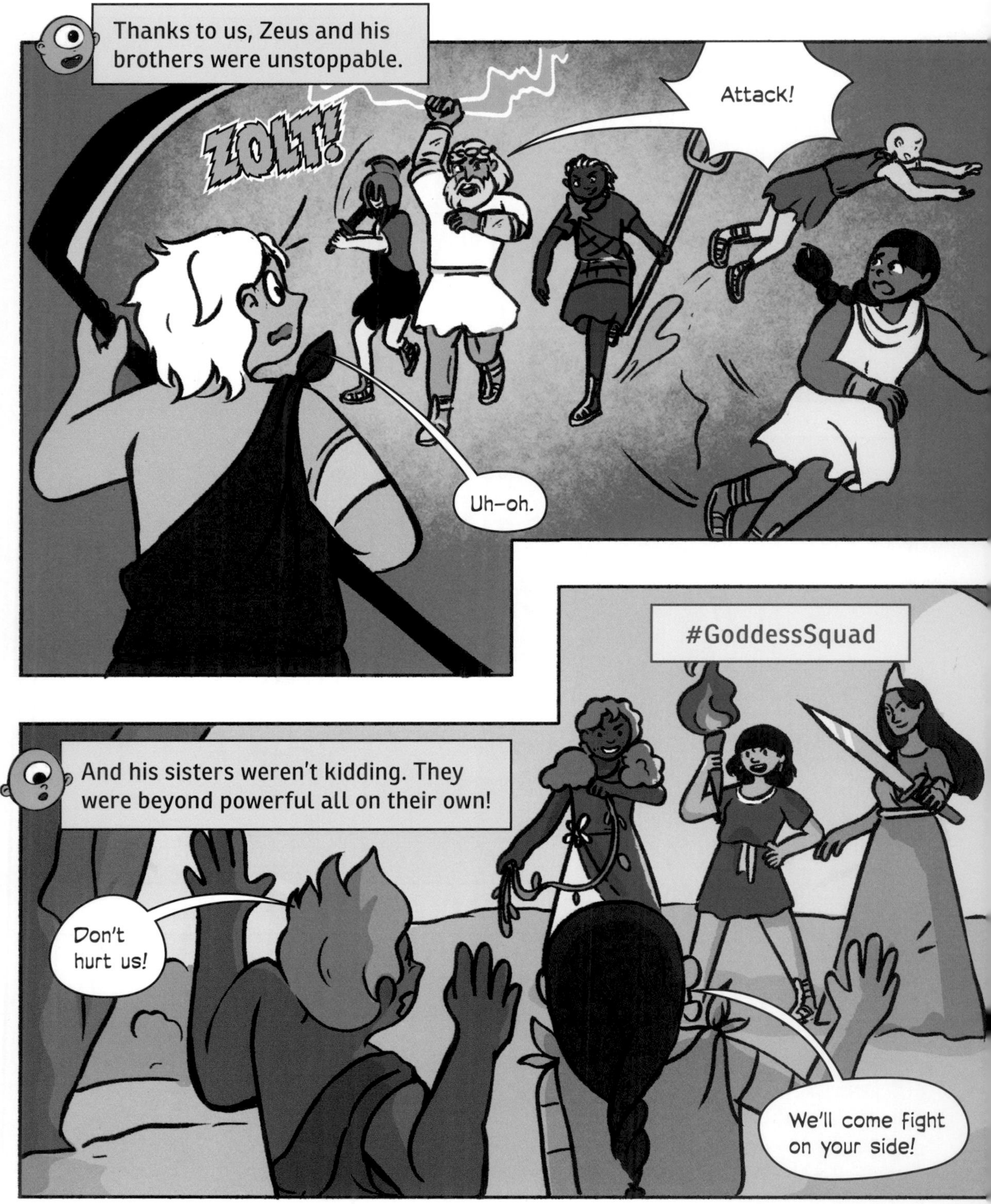

Thanks to us, Zeus and his brothers were unstoppable.
ZOLT!
Attack!
Uh-oh.
#GoddessSquad
And his sisters weren't kidding. They were beyond powerful all on their own!
Don't hurt us!
We'll come fight on your side!

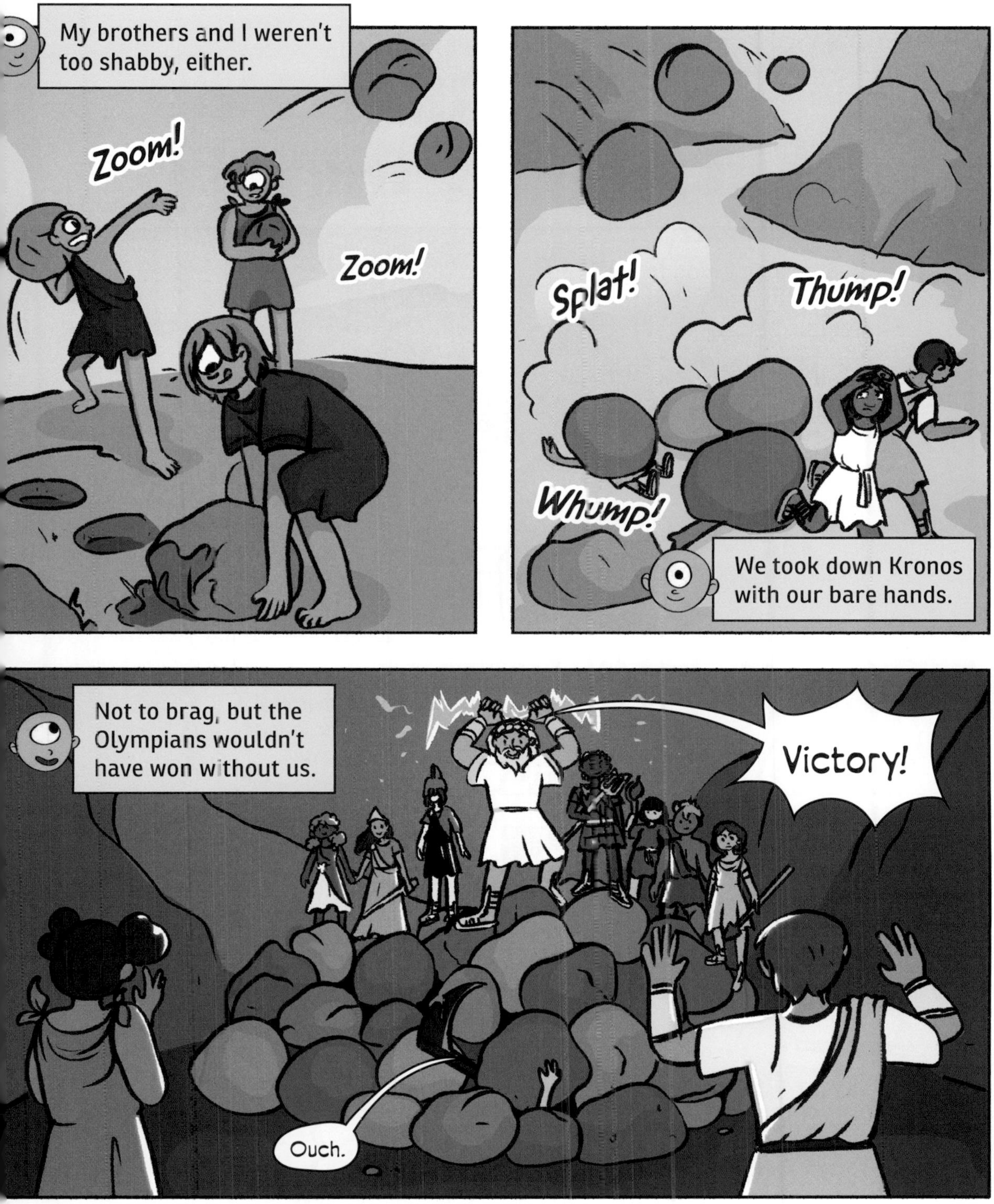

My brothers and I weren't too shabby, either.
Zoom!
Zoom!
Splat!
Thump!
Whump!
We took down Kronos with our bare hands.
Not to brag, but the Olympians wouldn't have won without us.
Victory!
Ouch.

CHAPTER 4

THE FINAL BATTLE . . . MAYBE!

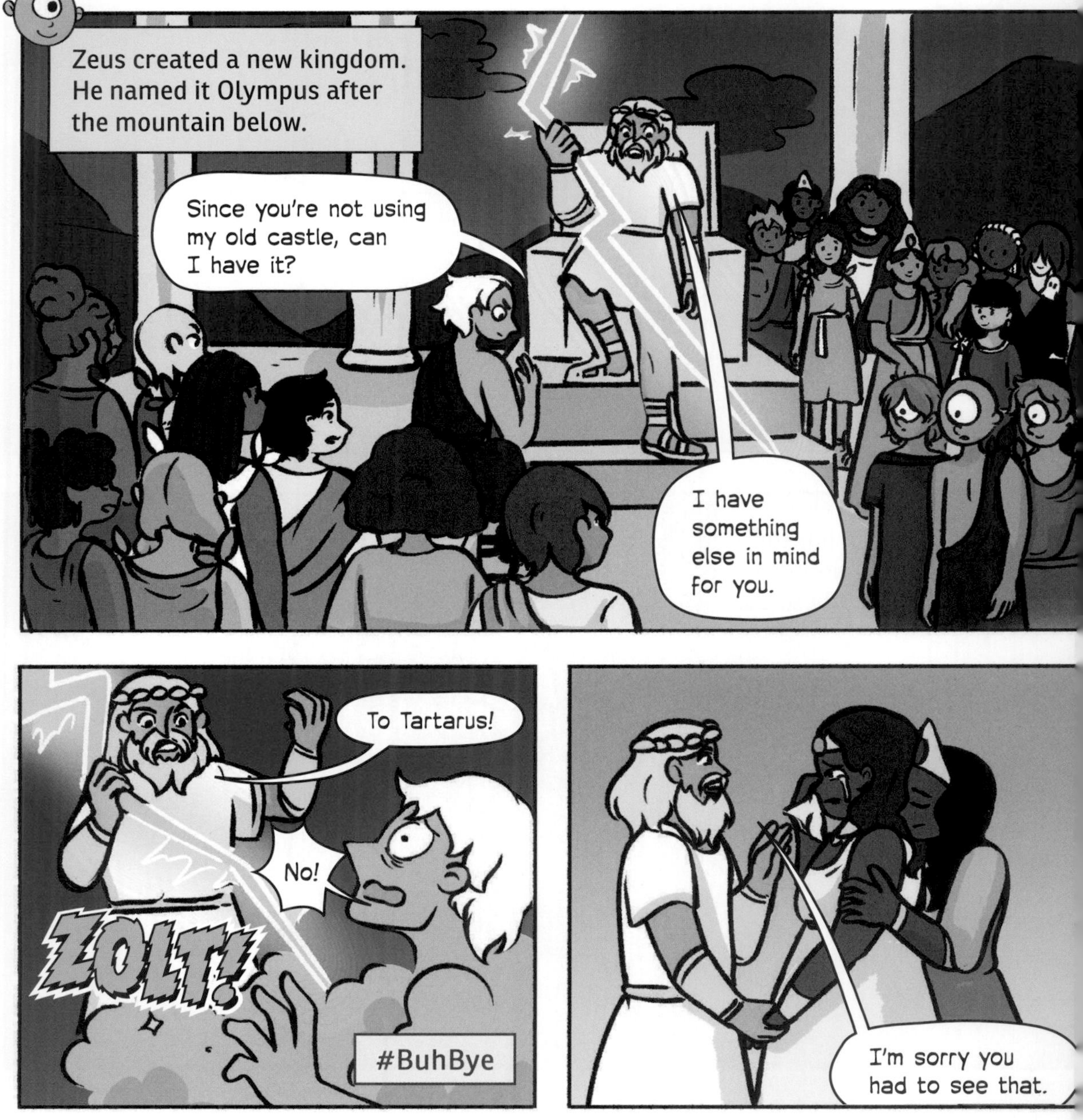
Zeus created a new kingdom. He named it Olympus after the mountain below.
Since you're not using my old castle, can I have it?
I have something else in mind for you.
To Tartarus!
No!
ZOLT!
#BuhBye
I'm sorry you had to see that.

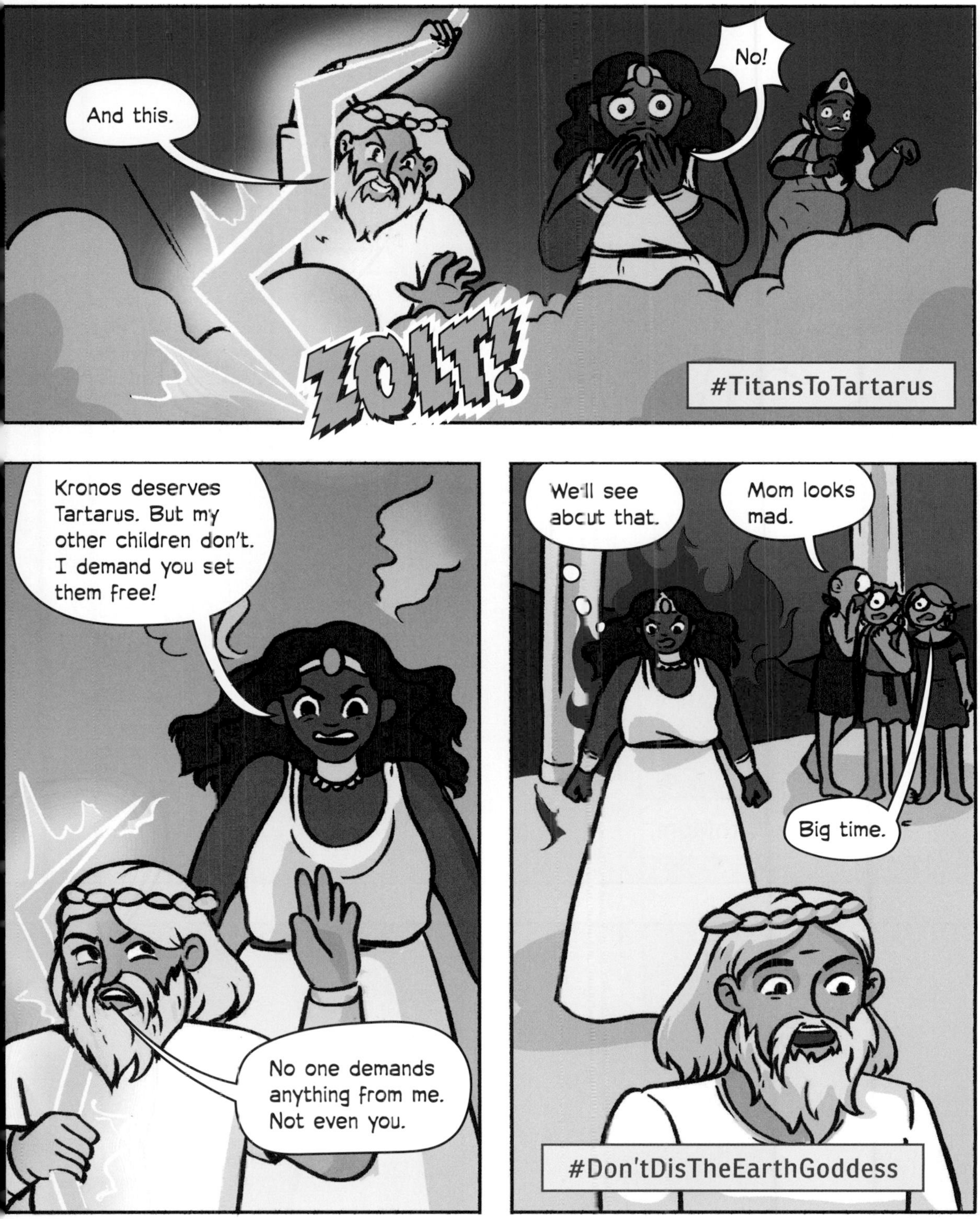
And this.
No!
ZOLT!
#TitansToTartarus
Kronos deserves Tartarus. But my other children don't. I demand you set them free!
No one demands anything from me. Not even you.
We'll see about that.
Mom looks mad.
Big time.
#Don'tDisTheEarthGoddess

Time passed. Zeus seemed to think Mom had forgotten about the Titans.

Meet my son, Hercules. He's a demigod—half human, half me.

I'll be a hero one day!

How nice for you.

But she hadn't.

Zeus trusts me now. It's time to put my plan into action. Soon my children will be free!

ZEUS WAS HERE

#Don'tMessWithMom

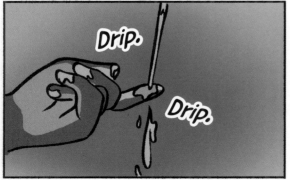

Drip.

Drip.

SPROING!

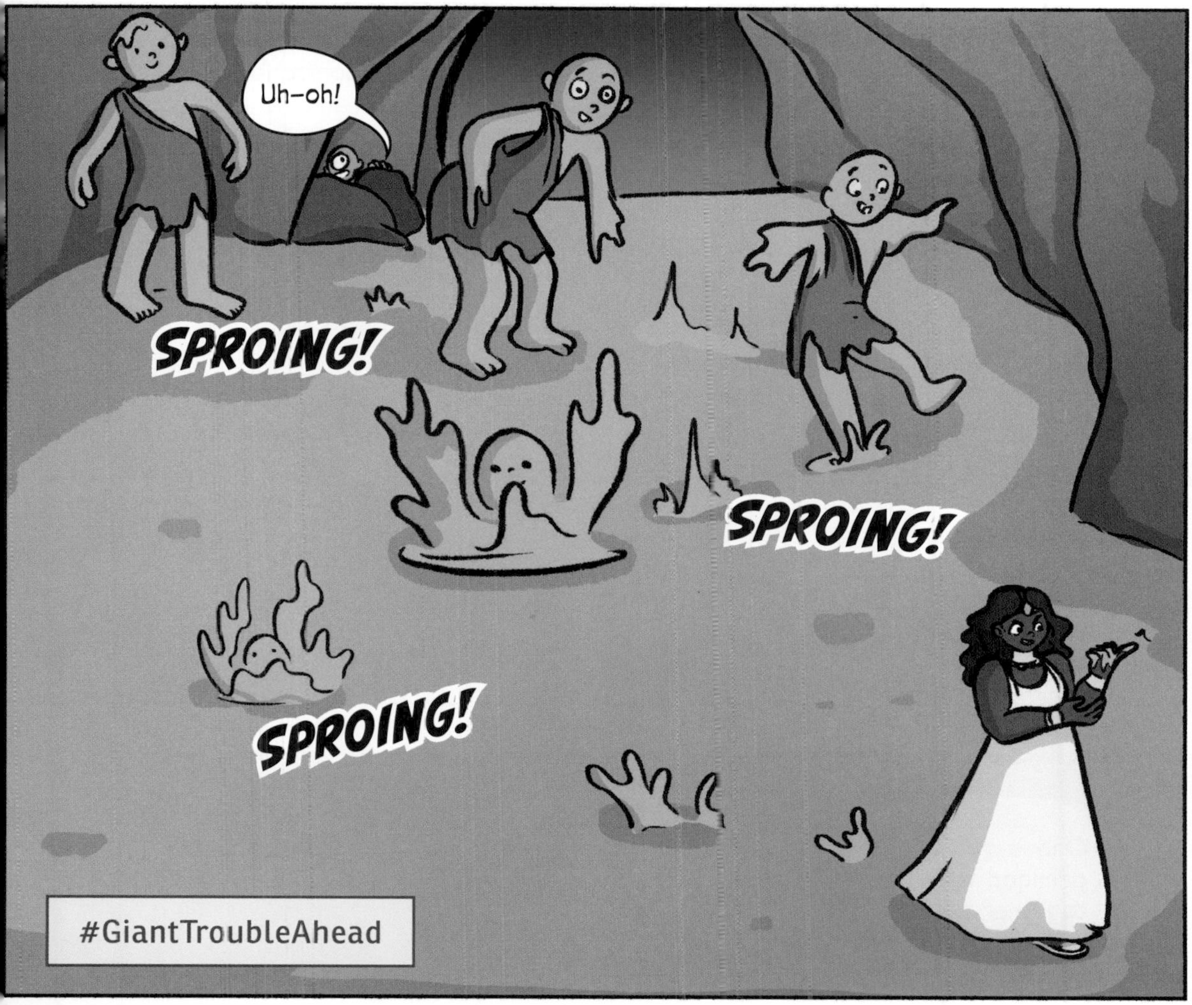
Uh-oh!
SPROING!
SPROING!
SPROING!
#GiantTroubleAhead

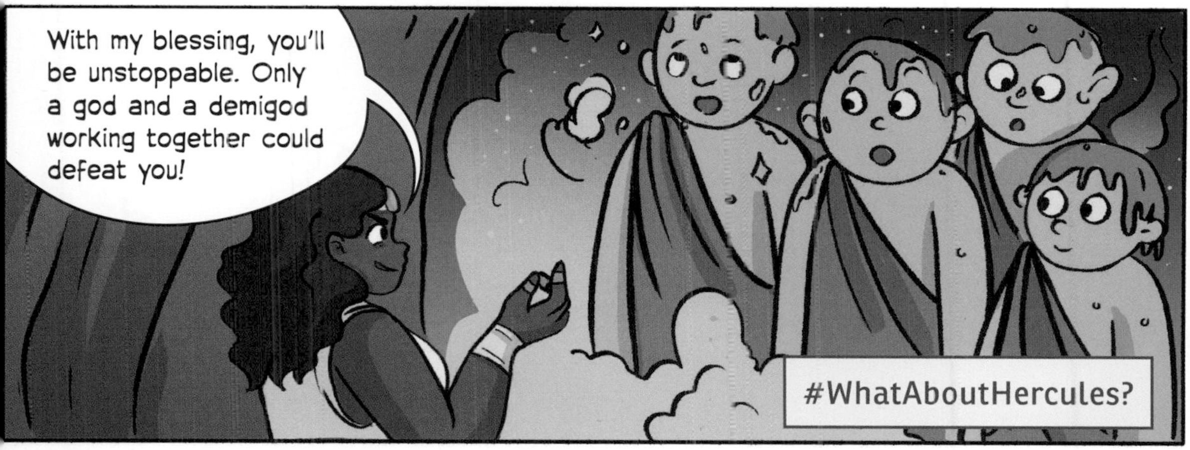
With my blessing, you'll be unstoppable. Only a god and a demigod working together could defeat you!
#WhatAboutHercules?

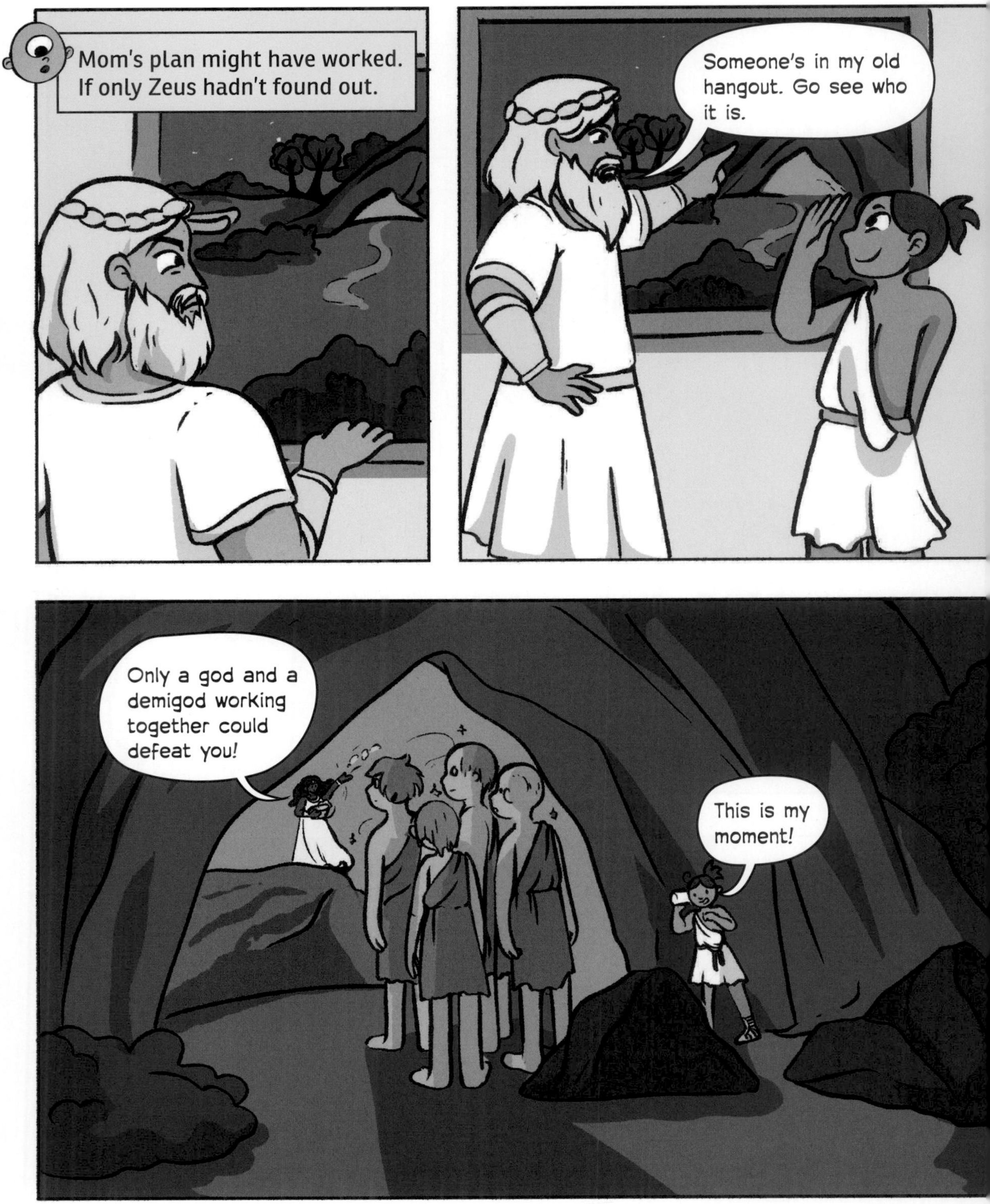
Mom's plan might have worked. If only Zeus hadn't found out.
Someone's in my old hangout. Go see who it is.
Only a god and a demigod working together could defeat you!
This is my moment!

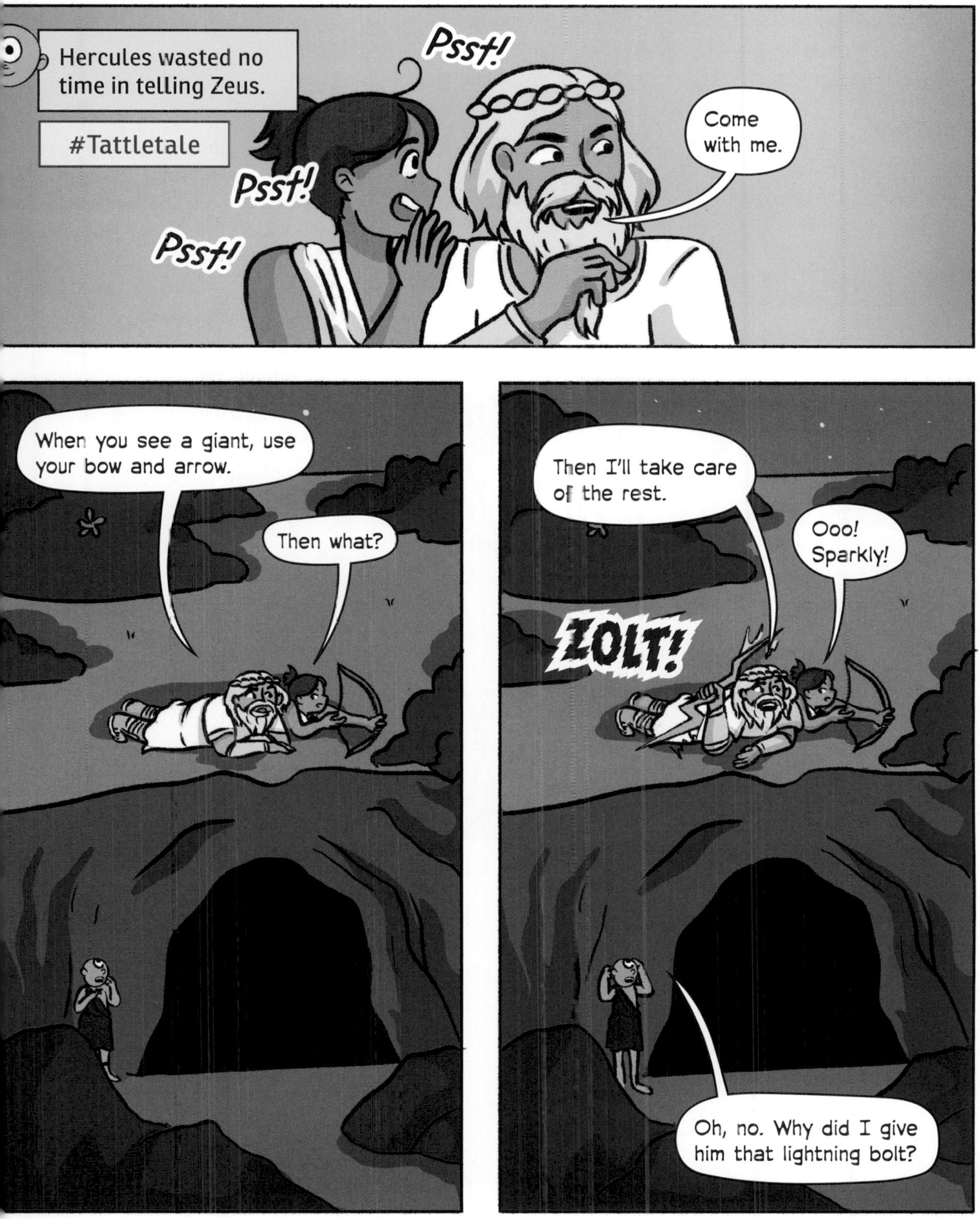
Hercules wasted no time in telling Zeus.
#Tattletale
Psst!
Psst!
Psst!
Come with me.
When you see a giant, use your bow and arrow.
Then what?
Then I'll take care of the rest.
Ooo! Sparkly!
ZOLT!
Oh, no. Why did I give him that lightning bolt?

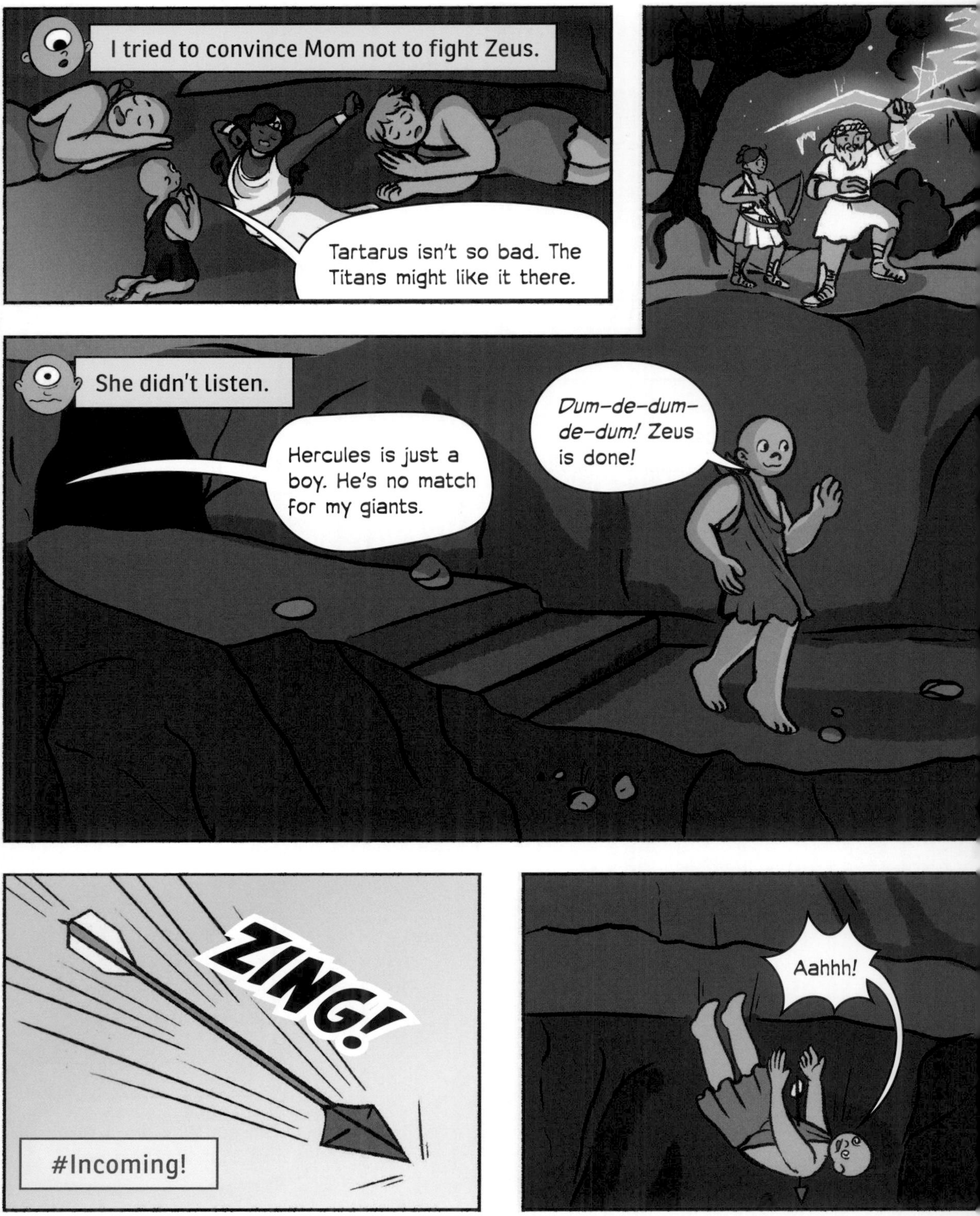
I tried to convince Mom not to fight Zeus.
Tartarus isn't so bad. The Titans might like it there.
She didn't listen.
Hercules is just a boy. He's no match for my giants.
Dum-de-dum-de-dum! Zeus is done!
ZING!
#Incoming!
Aahhh!

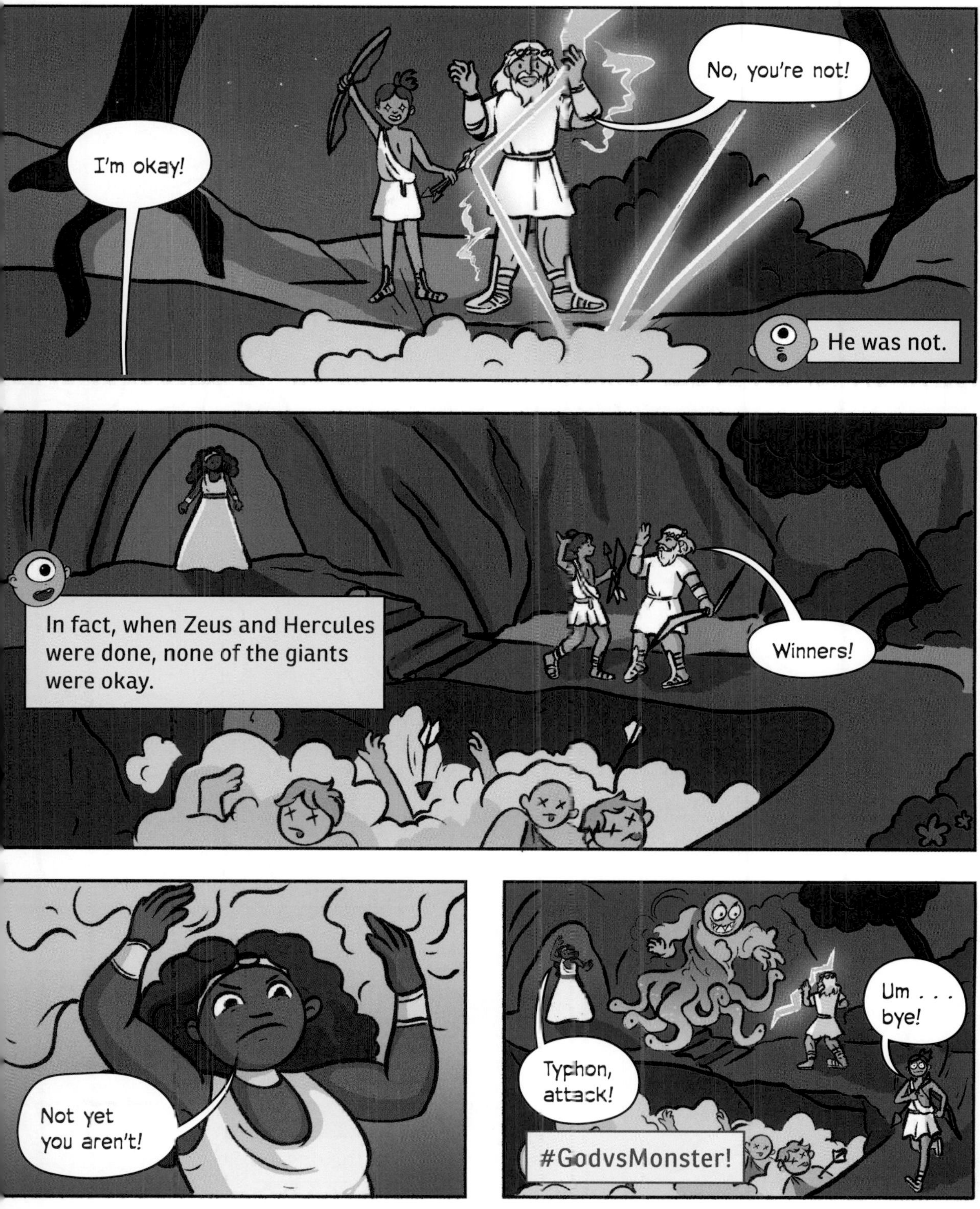

I'm okay!
No, you're not!
He was not.
In fact, when Zeus and Hercules were done, none of the giants were okay.
Winners!
Not yet you aren't!
Typhon, attack!
Um . . . bye!
#GodvsMonster!

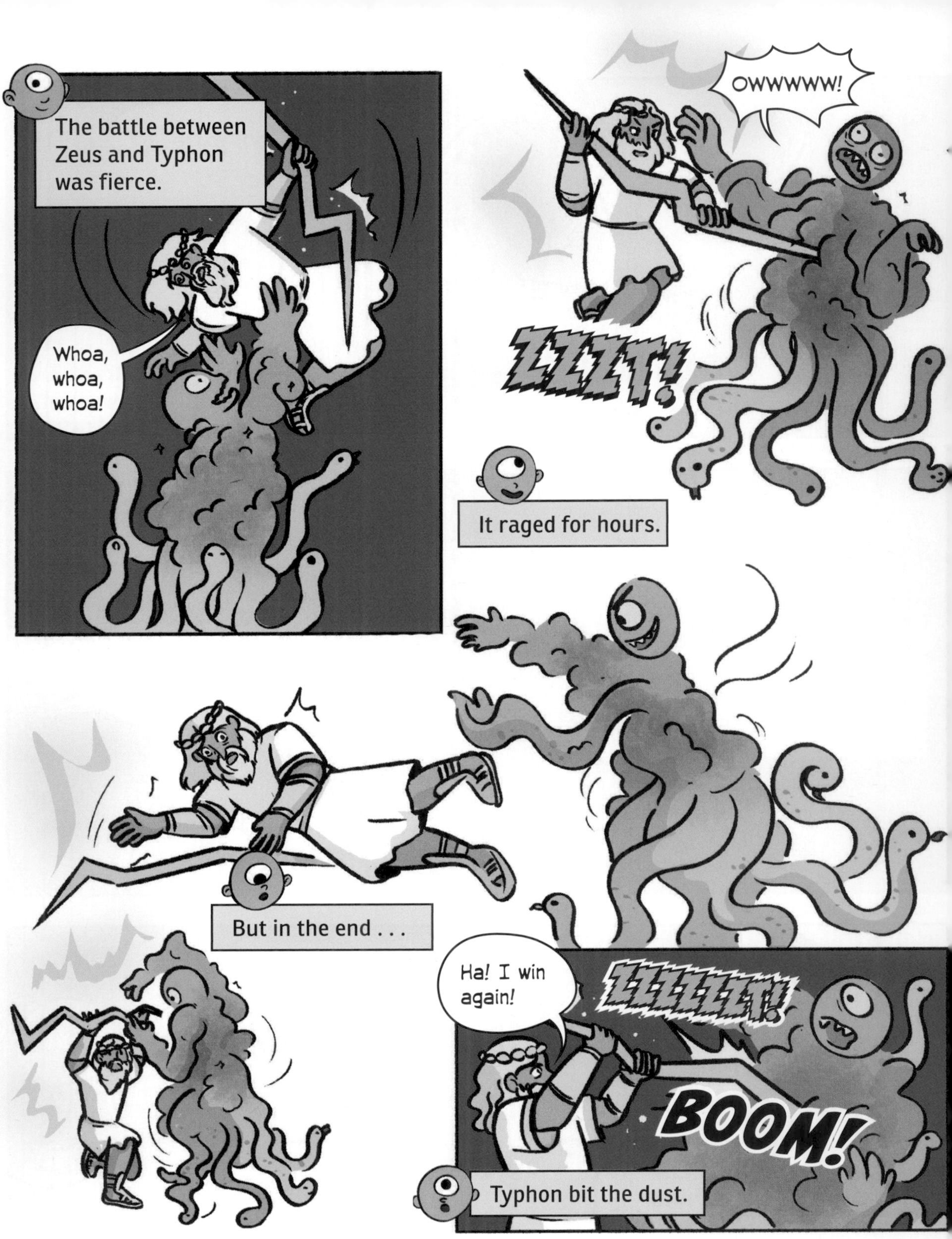
The battle between Zeus and Typhon was fierce.
Whoa, whoa, whoa!
OWWWWW!
ZZZT!
It raged for hours.
But in the end . . .
Ha! I win again!
ZZZZZZT!
BOOM!
Typhon bit the dust.

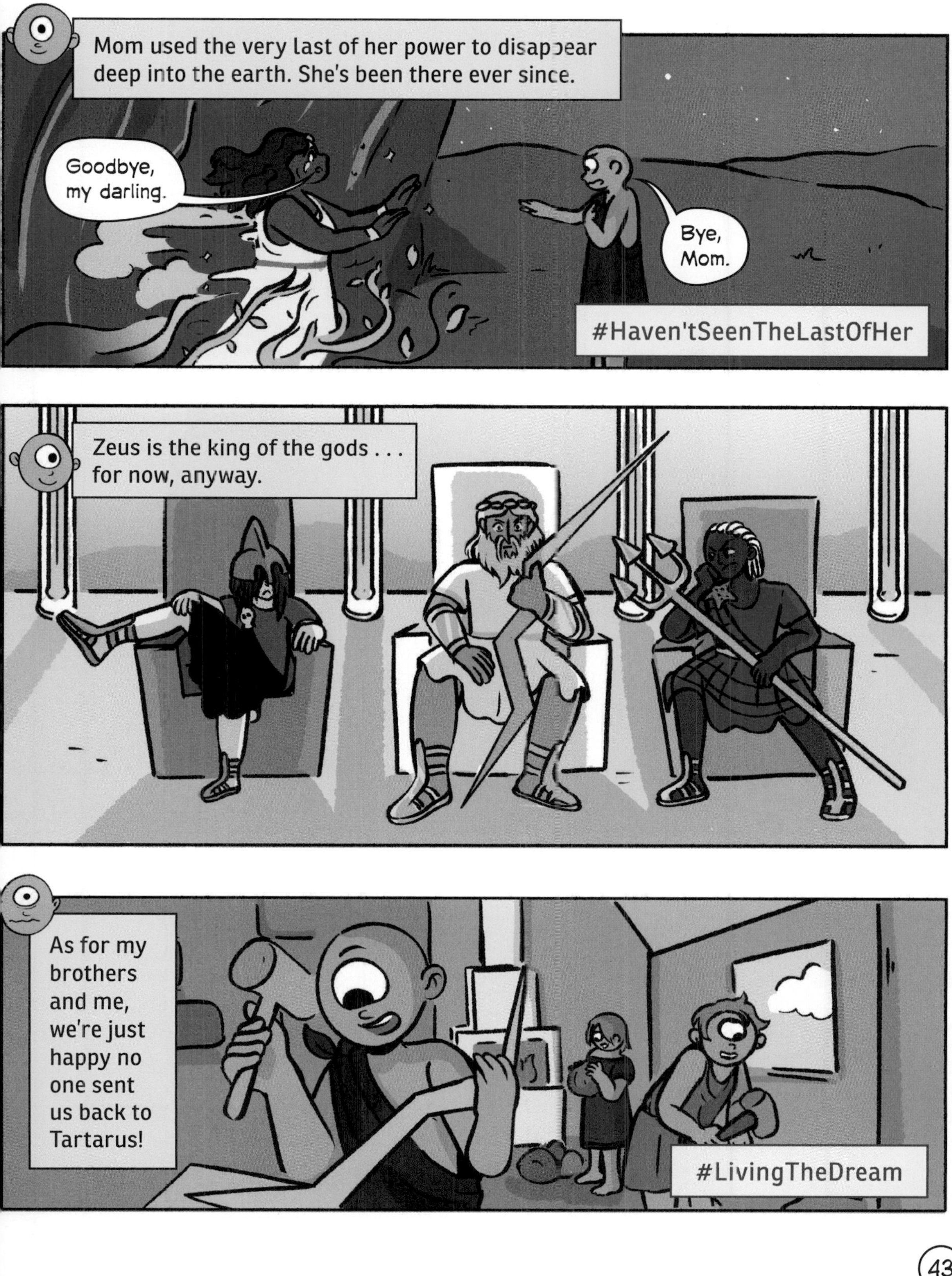
Mom used the very last of her power to disappear deep into the earth. She's been there ever since.
Goodbye, my darling.
Bye, Mom.
#Haven'tSeenTheLastOfHer
Zeus is the king of the gods . . . for now, anyway.
As for my brothers and me, we're just happy no one sent us back to Tartarus!
#LivingTheDream

More About the Battle of the Titans

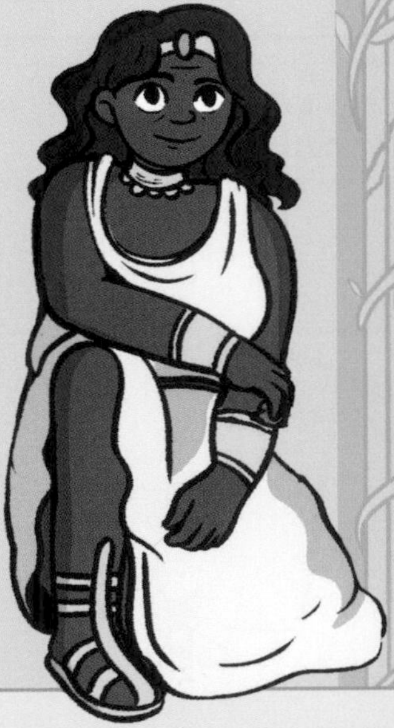

Gaia is the earth goddess. She is the mother of the Titans and grandmother of the Olympians. She's also known as the mother goddess because she created everything on Earth.

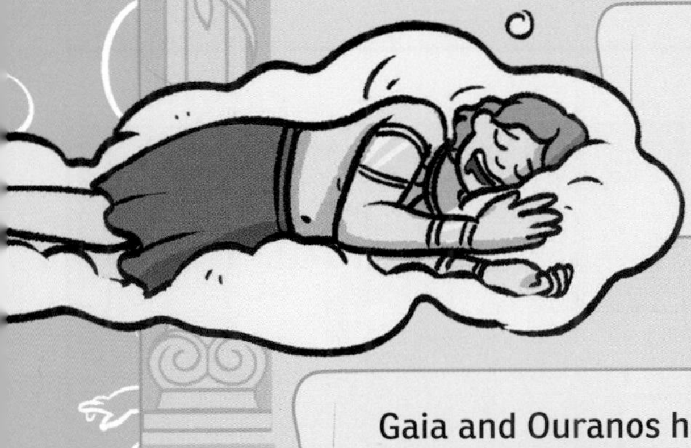

Ouranos is the sun god. He is the father of the Titans and grandfather of the Olympians. The planet Uranus is named after him.

Gaia and Ouranos had three other children too. They were called the Hundred-Handed Ones or the Hundred-Handers. Each one had 50 heads and 100 hands!

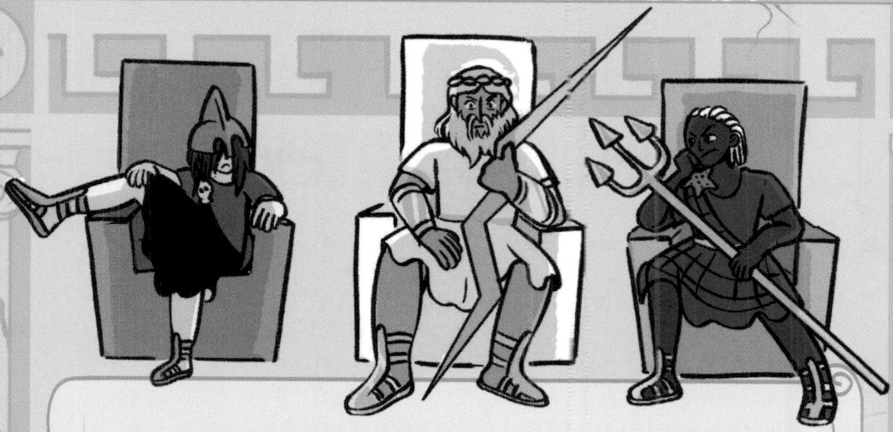

After defeating the Titans, Zeus and his brothers Poseidon and Hades divided up the world. Zeus ruled the sky. Poseidon ruled the oceans. Hades controlled the Underworld, also known as the land of the dead.

One of the Titans, Atlas, didn't end up in Tartarus with the rest of his siblings. Instead, Zeus made him hold the universe on his shoulders—forever!

According to some myths, a goat helped raise baby Zeus. One of the goat's horns had the power to give the holder whatever they wanted. It became known as a cornucopia—a horn of plenty.

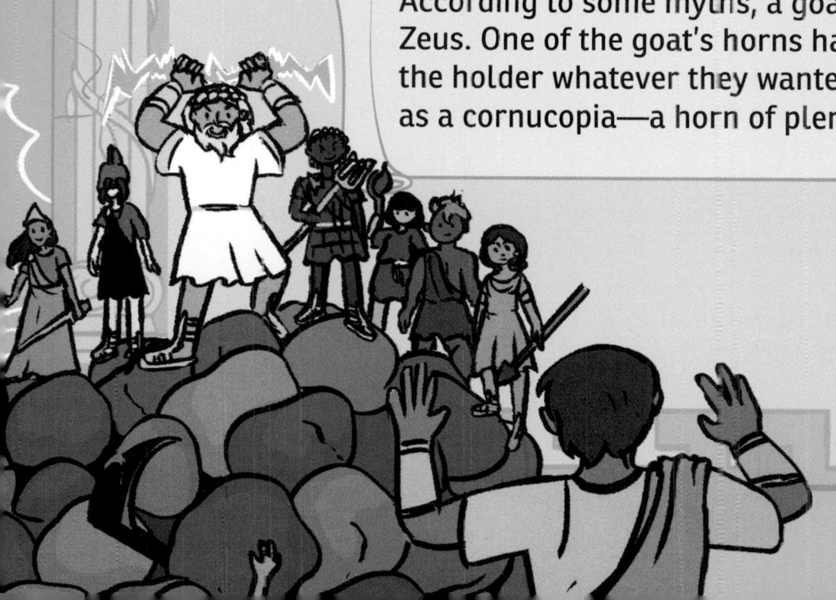

GLOSSARY

banish (BAN-ish)—to send away forever

Cyclops (SAHY-klops)—a one-eyed giant

deities (DEE-uh-tees)—gods or goddesses

epic (EP-ik)—long or great in size or scope

Gaia (GEY-uh)—in Greek mythology, the Earth goddess and mother of the Cyclopes and Titans

Hades (HEY-deez)—the Greek god of the Underworld

Olympian (uh-LIM-pee-uhn)—one of the Greek gods living on Olympus

Olympus (uh-LIM-puhs)—the highest mountain in Greece; in Greek mythology, the home of the Greek gods

Othrys (OTH-ris)—a high mountain in Greece; in Greek mythology, the home of the Titans

Ouranos (oo-REY-nuhs)—in Greek mythology, the first god of the sky and father of the Cyclopes and Titans

Poseidon (poh-SAHY-duhn)—the Greek god of the sea

sickle (SIK-uhl)—a tool with a long, curved blade attached to a short handle

Tartarus (TAHR-ter-uhs)—a mythical underground pit used as a prison

Titan (TYE-tuhn)—one of a family of giants overthrown by the gods of ancient Greece

INTERNET SITES

Britannica Kids: Titans
kids.britannica.com/kids/article/Titans/353864

Ducksters: Greek Mythology: The Titans
www.ducksters.com/history/ancient_greece/titans.php

Kids Love Greece: Greek Mythology for Kids: Greek Gods, Their Symbols and Temples in Greece
www.kidslovegreece.com/en/greece_online/greek-mythology-for-kids-greek-gods-their-symbols-and-temples-in-greece/

BOOKS IN THIS SERIES

MYTHOLOGY GRAPHICS
BATTLE OF THE TITANS
MYTHOLOGY GRAPHICS
THE CURSE OF MEDUSA
MYTHOLOGY GRAPHICS
JASON AND THE ARGONAUTS
MYTHOLOGY GRAPHICS
PANDORA'S BOX
MYTHOLOGY GRAPHICS
PERSEPHONE AND THE UNDERWORLD
MYTHOLOGY GRAPHICS
THESEUS AND THE MINOTAUR
MYTHOLOGY GRAPHICS
THE TROJAN HORSE
MYTHOLOGY GRAPHICS
THE TWELVE LABORS OF HERCULES

ABOUT THE CREATORS

Stephanie Peters has been writing books for children for more than 25 years. Her most recent Capstone titles include *The Unusual Journey from Pebbles to Continents: A Graphic Novel About Earth's Land* as well as *The Twelve Labors of Hercules: A Modern Graphic Greek Myth* and *The Trojan Horse: A Modern Graphic Greek Myth* in the Mythology Graphics series. An avid reader, workout enthusiast, and beach wanderer, Stephanie enjoys spending time with her family and their pets. She lives and works in Mansfield, Massachusetts.

Marian Sloane is a children's illustrator and graphic artist with a love for creating work on themes of friendship, found family, and LGBTQ+ characters. Marian works digitally and likes adding as many plants as possible.